RACE, GENDER, AND CRIMINAL JUSTICE

Equality and Justice for All?

Edited by

Danielle McDonald and Alexis Miller
Northern Kentucky University

 cognella
San Diego, CA

Bassim Hamadeh, CEO and Publisher
Christopher Foster, General Vice President
Michael Simpson, Vice President of Acquisitions
Jessica Knott, Managing Editor
Stephen Milano, Creative Director
Kevin Fahey, Cognella Marketing Program Manager
Becky Smith, Acquisitions Editor
Sarah Wheeler, Project Editor
Brian Fahey, Licensing Associate

16 15 14 13 12   1 2 3 4 5

Printed in the United States of America

ISBN: 978-1-60927-180-0

www.cognella.com 800.200.3908

CONTENTS

SECTION 1: UNDERSTANDING RACE AND GENDER

Chapter One: Race and Ethnicity   3
By Christian L. Bolden

Chapter Two: The Four Dimensions of Gender   17
By Jeffrey Cohen and Randy Martin

SECTION 2: RACE, GENDER, AND POLICING

Chapter Three: Racial Profiling   37
By Travis Humkey

Chapter Four: Policing and the War on Drugs   53
By Danielle McDonald

SECTION 3: RACE, GENDER, AND THE COURTS

Chapter Five: Specialized Courts   67
By Michael Bush

Chapter Six: Prosecutorial Discretion   87
By Isis N. Walton and Shanieka S. Jones

SECTION 4: RACE, GENDER, AND CORRECTIONS

Chapter Seven: Justice, War, and the Incarceration Boom   107
By Cheryl Lero Jonson

Chapter Eight: Arbitrariness and Disparities in the
Administration of the Death Penalty   125
By Diana Falco

SECTION 5: RACE, GENDER, THE EX OFFENDER, AND THE COMMUNITY

Chapter Nine: Inmate Reentry   141
By Richard Tewksbury and David Patrick Connor

Chapter Ten: Disenfranchisement   159
By Cherie Dawson Edwards

DEDICATION

Danielle McDonald

*To my husband and best friend Charles Scott for
always believing in me and our son Charles Paul
who reminds me each day why we should all continue
to strive for justice and equality.*

Alexis Miller

*To my lovely daughters, Anna and Addie,
without their love nothing would be worth the work.*

Section 1

Understanding Race and Gender

CHAPTER ONE

Race and Ethnicity

By Christian L. Bolden

Introduction

The concept of race is both real and imagined. That is to say, there are real differences in human appearance. People come in a myriad of skin colors, skin tones, and hair textures. The vast array of physical variations has often led people to imagine there are essential differences between people who look different that include everything from superiority to submissiveness to criminality. Even though scientific evidence has not supported these notions, the myths that are generated have continued to create strong beliefs, which sometimes turn into action. Despite the lack of factual evidence regarding the concept of race, people behave as if it were real, and therefore it becomes very real in its consequences. This is referred to as the social construction of reality (Henslin, 2010; Spickard, 1992; Thomas and Thomas, 1928).

That race is a socially constructed concept is supported by the inability of biological sciences to conclusively designate racial categories. Depending on which expert is asked, the answer to how many races there are could vary from one (human race), two (Caucasoid and Negroid), three (Caucasoid, Negroid, and Mongoloid) and so on up to 2,000 different groups (Montagu, 1964; 1999). A systematic investigation of human biology, which would determine the answer, has been undertaken. The Human Genome Project, a 13-year study that mapped DNA sequences of modern man, concluded that subspecies (races) do not exist (U.S. Department of Energy Genome Programs, 2007). This study has provided the world with a definitive answer to the question of race.

Accordingly, the American Anthropological Association (1998) issued a statement on race indicating that it has become clear that human populations are not unambiguous, clearly demarcated, biologically distinct groups. Evidence from the analysis of genetics (e.g., DNA) indicates that most physical variation, about 94%, lies within so-called racial groups. Conventional geographic "racial" groupings differ from one another only in about 6% of their genes. This means that there is greater variation within "racial" groups than between them.

Even though the evidence indicates that race is a social invention, the American Sociological Association emphasizes the importance of studying race due to people still behaving as if it were real. In a process referred to as **essentialism**, character traits are believed to be inherent in a particular racial group. These stereotypes can seemingly be benign, such as believing a group is superior at sports, or malicious, like believing a group is biologically criminal. Either way, these thought patterns ultimately lead to problematic relationships and discriminatory practices between groups.

The refusal to acknowledge race in official rhetoric does not mean that problems concerning race do not exist. For instance, policies of French and Brazilian governments were implemented that prevented or banned the collection of data on race, yet it was still found that systematic discrimination and inequality were prevalent in these countries (American Sociological Association, 2003). Trepagnier (2007) argues that it is the tacit aversion to discussing race that inadvertently allows for discriminatory practices to continue. Rhetorically, the issue of race at the individual level is sidestepped by proclamations such as "I am not racist," or explicitly avoiding the topic. However, refusing to address the issue does not mean that it will disappear.

For better or for worse, science is not typically used to designate racial categories. Instead, race is socially constructed by country or region. Each locale has its own formula for determining race, which may differ quite dramatically from other places. For instance, the group that is referred to as black or African American in the United States would be broken into different groups in Brazil: those with lighter skin and those with darker skin.

Why So Many Words?

Before we go any further, it is important to distinguish between the many words that are used when discussing the topic. **Race** is a reference to the physical description of a person or group of people. Despite the commonality of using this as a way to designate racial categories, the practice is prone to significant error, as members placed in these groups encompass vast variations in physical description. Another practice in designating racial categories is through the use of genetics. In this method, a person is placed in whichever category their parents or ancestors were placed in.

The term "race" is often confused or conflated with the word **ethnicity**, which refers to someone's cultural, national, and linguistic background. This could include the geographic place someone comes from, as well as the cultural trappings such as types of food and dress in those regions or a religious affiliation.

Finally, these words are often used interchangeably with the term "minority." Indeed, many racial and ethnic groups are minority groups but the terms do not have the same meaning. A **minority** group is made up of people who have less social power and privilege in a particular society. By this definition, physical and social categories of people who are disadvantaged in a society, such as those based on gender, disability, and sexual orientation, can be referred to as minority groups. Contrary to another definition of the word minority, when used in this context, it has nothing to do with numerical presence. In other words, a minority group could have a numerical majority yet still have less social power and privilege. An example of this would be South Africa during apartheid when black Africans vastly outnumbered whites who only made up 10% of the population, yet it was the white Africans who were the ruling power during that era. Groups that migrate or are forced to migrate to new countries often become minorities in the new location. If countries expand their own territories, then the people in the new territory also become minorities. For example, once Israel gained the Gaza Strip and West Bank through various wars, the Palestinians living in these areas became minorities.

Members of the **dominant** group, or group in power, often devalue the physical and cultural traits of minority groups. Consequently, members of minority groups tend to suffer from discrimination, are less likely to marry outside of their particular group (Wagley and Harris, 1958), and are more likely to participate in events aimed at promoting solidarity, such as ethnic holidays and parades.

Classifications in the United States

The process of racial/ethnic categorization in the United States is a prime example of how the concepts are socially constructed. U.S. categories have changed quite significantly over time. According to the U.S. census, there are five racial categories: White, Black/African American, Native American/Alaskan Native, Asian, and Native Hawaiian/Other Pacific Islander. The census further recognizes two ethnicities: Hispanic/Latino and Non-Hispanic/Latino (Census, 2010). It is important to note that the U.S. Census Bureau recognizes that its categories are social rather than biological.

Black/African American is a category that consists of people whose ancestry derives from black groups in Africa (Census, 2010). The violent and unjust treatment of blacks in the United States during slavery and the Jim Crow era was reflected in the categorization process. Historically, the one-drop rule was used, which meant that genetically, one drop of black blood categorized an individual as black (Hickman, 1997). This rule developed due to the number of mixed children produced from slave owners having sex with or raping their slaves. During this time, blacks were not allowed to inherit or own property. By classifying the mixed children as black, no property could be inherited from their fathers. While this rule seems unjust, antiquated, and preposterous from a modern perspective, it has appeared and been enforced as late as 1982. In Louisiana that year, a woman by the name of Susie Phipps, who for all intents and purposes thought of herself as white, found out that government documents had her listed as black. When she petitioned to have this designation changed, the courts fought her, traced her ancestry back and discovered that she was 1/32nd black. The courts ruled against her. It is important to note that this and other racial categories lump people together who have significant cultural differences. In this case, Africans, African Americans, Cape Verdeans, and West Indians—all with vastly different histories and cultural trappings—are placed in the same category.

Native American groups stem from the original inhabitants of the American continents. Tribes have been allowed to stipulate their own conditions of inclusion as Native American (Census, 2010). Acceptable Native American ancestry can range from one quarter to one sixteenth. Some groups stipulate that people with partial black ancestry will be excluded regardless of the amount of Native American ancestry.

Pacific Islanders include people with origins in Hawaii, Guam, Samoa, Chamorro, or other islands in the Pacific. Asians as a category include people with ancestry from the Far East, Southeast Asia, the Indian subcontinent, Japan, the Philippines, and Indonesian Islands.

Many of the people now considered white in the United States at some point would not have been considered as such. The English and German settlers in the United States were considered white; however, other ethnic groups such as the Irish, Polish, Italians, and people from southern and eastern Europe, were not included and indeed were discriminated against. Over time, these groups began to lose their ethnic identities by adapting to the English language and customs. Once they were assimilated they became a part of the dominant group and were referred to as white. Now, "white" refers to people whose ancestry stems from Europe, the Middle East, or northern Africa (Census, 2010). Multiracial options became available beginning with the 2000 census. Prior to this, respondents had to check one box; now they may check as many boxes as they choose to identify their racial background.

The United States recognizes two ethnicities: Hispanic/Latino or non-Hispanic/Latino. Prior to 1970, these ethnic choices were not recognized and Hispanics were considered white. In 1930 there was an attempt to create the racial category of "Mexican" on the census. The Mexican government and people of Mexican descent in the United States strongly resisted losing their status as white and successfully campaigned to have this category removed before the next census (Foley, 2005). However, it was only a matter of time before the U.S. government again attempted to make a distinction between this group and other whites. In the 1970 census, Congress wanted to create a designation that recognized people with a Spanish-speaking background; thus, the category "Hispanic" came into existence. Although the terms Hispanic and Latino are used interchangeably, there is technically a difference. Hispanic refers to someone who has origins in a Spanish-speaking culture, whereas Latino refers to someone with origins in Latin America (Central America, South America, some Caribbean Islands). Certain countries in Latin America, such as Brazil, are not Spanish speaking; therefore, they consider themselves Latino but not Hispanic.

It is important to recognize that Hispanic/Latino is an ethnicity, not a race. People of this cultural background can be of any race—black, white, Asian, or Native American. Many Latinos who have brown skin tones are thought to be mestizo (white and Native American), Afro-mestizo (black and Native American, or mulatto (black and white). However, in the United States, the majority of Latinos designate their race as white.

Measuring Race/Ethnicity in Other Countries

Many countries in the world have a categorization system for race and ethnicity, yet not all of them record information on the subject. For those that do, there is no universal way to go about it, as conceptions of racial/ethnic groups vary and could be described as nationalities, tribes, or designations such as indigenous or aboriginal. The criteria for categorical systems could be based on one factor such as skin color (e.g., South African-white, colored or mixed race, Asian, African) to very complex variations (e.g., Brazil, which uses a combination of skin color, ancestry, and social class). Studies of census information collected by the United Nations on 87 countries that do collect this data indicate that 49 (56%) of these countries categorize by *ethnic group* or combination of ethnic group with other terms such as caste, dialect, *nationality*, and race. The measurement that ranked second in frequency was nationality, which was used by 20 (23%) countries predominantly in eastern Europe or those that broke off of the former Soviet Union (Morning, 2008). The terms *indigenous* and *race* ranked equally in frequency of use, with 13 countries (15%) applying these designations. With the exception of one country in Africa, the terms indigenous and race were used exclusively on the American continents and Oceania.

Examining the method of measurement in the United States from a global perspective reveals that it is one of only 13 countries that use the term race;

Box 1-1. Race and Ideology in Global Court

In September 2011, a judge in South Africa ruled that singing the lyrics of a particular rap song called *Shoot the Boer* qualified as hate speech and therefore was illegal. The song was popular amongst Africans during apartheid and the words refer to violently responding to the crimes of Boers (whites, especially Dutch Afrikaners). The ruling came from a suit against Julius Malema, a leader of the youth league of the African National Congress party, who would publicly sing the song. The judge argued that the ruling was necessary to help heal a country that has been torn by ethnic strife and hopes that it will allow the different sides to begin a dialogue and learn about each other(Bryson, 2011). What do you think? Will quashing hate speech help to resolve ethnic divisions, or will the result be very different? How would this scenario play out in the United States?

it is the only country that distinguishes race from ethnicity; and it is the only country that uses ethnicity to single out only one group: Hispanics (Morning, 2008).

Racial Ideologies and Criminological Thinking

As previously stated, even though race is an imagined concept, it has had very real and dramatic consequences. Belief in racial and ethnic superiority was common among people in most of the historical empires, including that of the Persians, Egyptians, Greeks, Romans, and British. The assumption of cultural superiority included the idea that other groups must be inherently inferior. These **ideologies**, or beliefs that this is the natural order of things, led to the notion that it was the burden of "civilized" peoples to tame those of other cultures who were considered brutish and savage, thus justifying systems of stratification such as slavery or colonial societies. A **colonial system** is one in which one country conquers another and implements economic and political subjugation. The invading country is usually after the natural resources and uses the subjugated people as an unskilled workforce to obtain those resources. A set of philosophical and rhetorical arguments is used to reinforce the ideology that the dominant-subordinate positions are inherent and natural (Marger, 2009). Famous philosophers such as Immanuel Kant believed that racial superiority was a fundamental truth and that blacks were so mentally inferior that even if they were set free they would not develop any talent (Kant, 2004).

Another relationship pattern that has been justified by racial ideologies is ethnic cleansing, or **genocide**, in which one group attempts to eradicate another. In this scenario, one group takes an extreme interpretation of survival of the fittest, and authorizes the elimination of another group that is perceived to be inferior. The most well-known example of this was the genocide of six million Jews by the Nazi regime. There have also been several other instances of this pattern, including the killing of nearly one million Tutsi by the Hutu in Rwanda, and the massacre of one million Cambodians by the Khmer Rouge, with the victims mostly being ethnic minorities (Kiernan, 1996; Prunier, 1995)

Before racial ideologies were scientifically challenged, they were taken for granted among scientific disciplines and assumed as truth. Criminology was no exception to this and incorporated racial ideologies from its inception. Cesare Lombroso (1835–1909), often referred to as "the father of criminology," believed that man's behavior was genetically determined. Criminals, according to Lombroso, could be described as "atavistic," or genetic throwbacks to early evolutionary versions of man. Atavism was believed to be apparent through the physical characteristics of a man, such as facial structures and musculature. Thus the atavistic man appeared simian and was common among what Lombroso referred to as the lower races of man.

> We find anatomical peculiarities, which in some cases resemble the characters of the few authentic remnants of the earliest historical beings, in other cases correspond to the still extant lower races of mankind, and in yet others, correspond to the characters of some or all of the varieties of monkey (Kurella, 1910:21)

Although much of his work focused on the physical appearance of the atavistic criminal, Lombroso also stressed the importance of race. In some cases he described entire cultures as being criminal in nature.

> There exist whole tribes of races more or less given to crime, such as the tribe Zakka Khel in India. In all regions of Italy, whole villages constitute hot-beds of crime, owing, no doubt, to ethnical causes … The frequency of homicide in Calabria, Sicily, and Sardinia is fundamentally due to African and Oriental elements. In the gypsies

we have an entire race of criminals with all the passions and vices common to delinquent types (Lombroso-Ferrero, 1911).

Earnest Albert Hooton (1887–1954) continued the Lombrosian tradition of racial biological determinism in regard to criminality. Hooten's primary argument was that criminals were physically inferior and that race was one of the determinants in what type of crime a person would commit:

> Differences in constitutional type, whether of racial origin or due to familial or individual factors of endocrine or other causation undoubtedly are agents in determining the choice of offense (Hooton, 1939: 308).

Hooton and other biological determinists fell out of favor as sociologists and criminologists uncovered evidence that crime was ecologically related to geographical locations, regardless of what racial or ethnic group occupied the area. Even after particular groups transitioned out of a high-crime area and a new group took their place, criminal activity in that area would still be significant. As ecological and subcultural explanations took hold in the 1930s and 1940s, mainstream criminologists abandoned biological determinism. Although there has been a resurgence of biological theories in modern criminology, racial determinism is not involved. Modern theories focus on psychological, physiological, and hormonal interactions with environmental stimuli that may affect behavior.

Racial Criminal Justice in the United States

From the inception of slavery in the United States, there was a different system of justice for blacks and whites. Black codes or slave codes penalized people for being black. Behaviors such as failing to accommodate a white person could result in severe penalties. If a black person harmed a white person, attempted to revolt, or had sex with a white woman, the penalty would be death. Russell (1998) explains that these behaviors threatened the existing social system and thus were punished more severely. Furthermore, if a slave attempted to escape, a part of the person's body would be amputated and posted as a warning to other slaves. Slaves did not receive legal representation, jury trials, appeals, or even the presumption of innocence (Russell, 1998). Even though the slaves were freed after the Civil War, the Jim Crow laws that were instituted in the South kept this tiered system of justice, and in some aspects, made penalties for being black even harsher. As slaves, blacks were allowed to travel with whites and permitted in some of the same establishments. Under Jim Crow, blacks were barred from all public accommodations and facilities used by whites. During this legally enforced era, crimes committed by African Americans against other African Americans often went unpunished or were not dealt with harshly, as white Southerners deemed it expected or appropriate behavior (O'Brien, 1985).

Civil Rights Era

There were always people on both sides of the racial divide that challenged this dual system of justice. However, movement toward equalized justice did not gain momentum until the 1950s and 1960s. The civil rights era is often described in terms of tumultuous group relationships and unrest manifesting as protests, marches, freedom rides, sit-ins, and other forms of demonstration. The importance of these activities in propelling social change is unquestioned, yet the primary victories of that era were on the legal front, beginning with two major court cases in 1954. The first of these was *Brown v. the Board of Education of Topeka*. In this Supreme Court decision, the previous decision regarding separate but equal educational facilities in *Plessy v. Ferguson* (1896) was overturned. This unanimous ruling that segregated schools were inherently unequal paved the way for desegregation and is believed to be the official start of the civil rights era. In the same year, a suit resulting from the systematic exclusion of Mexican Americans from juries resulted in the Supreme Court case *Hernandez v. Texas* (1954). The Court ruled that the Fourteenth Amendment, which provides equal protection to citizens, applied to all nationality groups in the United States (Blumberg, 1984; Dudley, 1996; Sheridan, 2003).

Legal victories were not only limited to the courts, but were also seen in a series of legislative pieces passed by Congress. The Civil Rights Act of 1957, passed under President Dwight Eisenhower, created a Justice Department Civil Rights Division and attempted to protect voting rights. The subsequent Civil Rights Act of 1960 further strengthened federal investigative and punitive powers for tampering with voting registration and polls. The culmination of this series was the Civil Rights Act of 1964, passed under President Lyndon Johnson, which prohibited most forms of discrimination against blacks and women in employment, education, and public facilities. The act also created the Equal Employment Opportunity Commission (EEOC) (Blumberg, 1984; Dudley, 1996). The EEOC is a federal agency that investigates unfairness and bias in employment and enforces antidiscrimination laws. Finally, in 1967, President Johnson appointed Thurgood Marshall, the first African American Supreme Court justice.

Box 1-2. Mechanics of Oppression

Russell (1998) explained that threats to the social status quo of dominant groups were met with severe responses. A quick overview of prominent outspoken civil rights leaders paints a frightening picture. The motives of assailants may have varied but the overall result was quite devastating.

Civil Rights Leader	Position/Organization	Outcome	Date
Medgar Evers	NAACP Field Secretary	Assassinated	1963
John F. Kennedy	U.S. President	Assassinated	1963
Malcolm X	Nation of Islam	Assassinated	1965
Eldridge Cleaver	Black Panther (Oakland) Minister of Information	Exile	1968
Robert Kennedy	U.S. Senator	Assassinated	1968
Martin Luther King Jr.	Southern Christian Leadership Conference	Assassinated	1968
Huey P. Newton	Black Panther Founder	Incarcerated	1968
Stokely Carmichael	Student Nonviolent Coordinating Committee	Exile	1969
Bunchy Carter	Black Panther Founder (Southern California)	Assassinated	1969
Fred Hampton	Black Panther Chair (Illinois)	Assassinated	1969
Bobby Seale	Black Panther Founder	Incarcerated	1969

On the social front, organizations such as the Southern Christian Leadership Conference, the Student Nonviolent Coordinating Commission, and the Congress on Racial Equality were orchestrating sit-in protests at whites-only establishments, riding buses through the south while refusing to give up their seats to whites, and marching on state capitols where governments continued to support Jim Crow legal statutes. One such event marked a major turning point in civil rights. In 1963, thousands of protesters led by Martin Luther King Jr. marched on Birmingham, Alabama. They were met by police chief Bull Connor who unleashed police dogs and used water cannons and tear gas on the protestors. Much of this was televised and caused public sentiment to shift in favor of civil rights activists. Birmingham began to desegregate rapidly after this event (Blumberg, 1984; Dudley, 1996).

Within a seven-year span, nearly all of the major civil rights leaders—those who were militant and those who were peaceful—were gone. How do you think this scenario would affect the social psychology of a group? How would you feel if all of your heroes, all of the people who stood up for you, were eliminated?

The civil rights era technically ended by returning to the issue that initiated it: the desegregation of schools. The initial ruling in *Brown v. the Board of Education of Topeka* was that desegregation would occur with "all deliberate speed." This inadvertently encouraged the Southern states to implement stalling tactics, resulting in literal and metaphorical battlefields for civil rights. The Supreme Court redressed this in the *Swann v. Mecklenburg* ruling in 1969, that desegregation of schools happen universally and at once (Blumberg, 1984; Dudley, 1996).

Summary

An abundance of scientific evidence has been presented that demonstrates race/ethnicity as a social construct rather than biological reality. Genetic similarity between humans outweighs the slight differences. The differences that do exist are more pronounced *within* perceived groups than *between* perceived groups. That race/ethnicity is a social construction is also demonstrated on a global scale in that different countries have different categorical systems and conceptions of social grouping. Even so, these perceived differences result in very real behavior and tragic consequences. Surveying history reveals the use of racial ideologies to oppress, subjugate, enslave, and exterminate members of other groups. Racial ideologies have also been used to label entire racial/ethnic groups as inherently criminal. This has occurred throughout the world, including in the United States, where a racialized form of justice was used during slavery and in the Jim Crow South. Overcoming these beliefs, at least on the legal front, took a significant effort in the social, legal, and governmental arenas during the civil rights era.

References

American Anthropological Association. (1997). Statement on race. http://www.aaanet.org/stmts/racepp.htm

American Sociological Association. (2003). The importance of collecting data and doing social scientific research on race. Washington, DC: American Sociological Association. http://www2.asanet.org/media/asa_race_statement.pdf

Blumberg, R. L. (1984). *Civil Rights: The 1960s Freedom Struggle. Boston: Twayne. Brown v. the Board of Education of Topeka*, 347 U.S. 483 (1954).

Bryson, D. (2011). S. Africa rules against youth leader for hate speech. Associated Press. Retrieved Sep. 12, 2011.http://news.yahoo.com/safrica-rules-against-youth-leader-hate-speech-094521756.html

Civil Rights Act of 1964, Pub. L. No. 88-352, 78 Stat. 241.

Dudley, W. (ed.). (1996). *The Civil Rights Movement: Opposing Viewpoints*. San Diego: Greenhaven Press.

Henslin, J. M. (2010). *Race and Ethnicity in Sociology: A Down-to-Earth Approach*, 10th ed. Boston: Allyn & Bacon.

Hickman, C. B. (1997). The devil and the one-drop rule: Racial categories, African Americans, and the U.S. Census. *Michigan Law Review* 95, 1161–1265.

Hooton, E. A. (1939). *The American Criminal: An Anthropological Study*. Cambridge: Harvard University Press.

Foley, N. (2005). Becoming Hispanic: Mexican Americans and whiteness, in P. Rothenberg (ed.), *White Privilege*. New York: Worth.

Kant, I. (2004). *Observations on the Feeling of the Beautiful and the Sublime*.John T. Goldthwait (trans.).Berkeley: University of California Press.

Kiernan, B. (1996). *The Pol Pot Regime: Race, Power and Genocide in Cambodia under the Khmer Rouge, 1975–1979*. New Haven: Yale University Press.

Kurella, H. (1910). *Cesare Lombroso: A Modern Man of Science*. M. Eden Paul (trans.). New York: Rebman Company.

Lombroso-Ferrero, G. (1911). Criminal man, according to the classification of Cesare Lombroso. New York: G. P. Putnam.

Marger, M. N. (2009). *Race and Ethnic Relations: American and Global Perspectives*. Belmont, CA: Wadsworth.

Montagu, M. F. A. (1964). *The Concept of Race*. New York: Free Press.

Montagu, M. F. A. (ed.) (1999). *Race and IQ: Expanded Edition*. New York: Oxford University Press.

Morning, A.(2008). Ethnic classification in global perspective: A cross-national survey of the 2000 Census round. *Population Research and Policy Review* 27(2), 239–272.

O'Brien, R. N. (1985). Crime and victimization data. Beverly Hills, CA: Sage Publications. *Plessy v. Ferguson*, 163 U.S. 537 (1896).

Prunier, G. (1995). *The Rwandan Crisis: History of a Genocide*. New York: Columbia University Press.

Russell, K. K. (1998). *The Color of Crime: Racial Hoaxes, White Fear, Black Protectionism, Police Harassment, and Other Macroaggressions*. New York: University Press.

Sheridan, C. (2003). Another white race: Mexican Americans and the paradox of whiteness in jury selection. *Law and History Review* 21 (1), 109–144.

Spickard, P. R. (1992). The illogic of American racial categories, in M. P. Root (ed.), *Racially Mixed People in America*. Newbury Park, CA: Sage. *Swann v. Mecklenburg*, 402 U.S. 1 (1969).

Thomas, W. I., and Thomas, D. S. (1928). *The Child in America: Behavior Problems and Programs*. New York: Alfred A. Knopf.

Trepagnier, B. (2007). *Silent Racism: How Well-Meaning White People Perpetuate the Racial Divide*. Paradigm Publishers.

U.S. Census. (2010). Overview of race and Hispanic origin: 2010. Retrieved 2010. http://www.census.gov/prod/cen2010/briefs/c2010br-02.pdf

U.S. Department of Energy Genome Programs. (2007). Minorities, race, and genomics. Retrieved 2011. http://www.ornl.gov/sci/techresources/Human_Genome/elsi/minorities.shtml

Wagley, C., and Harris, M. (1958). *Minorities in the New World*. New York: Columbia: University Press.

Learn More on the Internet

Human Genome Project website:

   http://www.ornl.gov/sci/techresources/Human_Genome/home.shtml

Race and Ethnicity in the United States:

   http://factfinder.census.gov/servlet/ACSSAFFPeople?_submenuId=people_10&_sse=on

Slavery by Another Name: The Birth of Jim Crow Laws:

   http://video.pbs.org/video/2178294876

Discussion Questions

1. In the United States in the 1930s, an attempt was made to include "Mexican" as a racial category on the U.S. census questionnaire. Those of Mexican descent successfully fought this attempt and the racial category of Mexican was removed from the survey. Why did those of Mexican descent fight against being classified as Mexican rather than white?

2. Is there a difference between the biological understanding of race and the social construction of race? Does this distinction matter?

CHAPTER TWO

The Four Dimensions of Gender

By Jeffrey Cohen and Randy Martin

Introduction

This chapter is intended to provide an overview of gender as a social science construct and lived experience. The model we present is based on the application of **Integral Theory** (Wilber, 2006) and suggests that gender can be viewed through four distinct, yet interrelated, lenses. According to Esbjörn-Hargens (2006), "the Integral model is postdisciplinary in that it can be used successfully in the context of approaches considered *disciplinary* … *multidisciplinary*… *interdisciplinary* … and *transdisciplinary*" (p. 5; italics in original).

The model of gender presented in this chapter is disciplinary in that it draws on rigorous research from disciplines that have long been concerned with our understanding of gender, such as sociology, biology, and psychology. It is multidisciplinary in that it does not limit the discussion of gender to only one of these disciplines. Further, the model is interdisciplinary because it provides an overarching language of gender that can be used to communicate more clearly across disciplinary boundaries. Finally, it is transdisciplinary in that it creates the foundation for a discussion of gender that moves beyond our traditional disciplinary viewpoints. By bringing together theories from a variety of disciplinary lenses, we are better able to understand the complexity of gender as both a social science construct and lived experience.

Gender Dichotomies

Traditionally, gender has been dichotomized in two distinct ways. Many people are familiar with the dichotomy between **gender** and **sex.** Within this particular dichotomy, sex is broadly defined as biological differences and gender is broadly defined as differences ascribed by society (see Belknap, 2007). Another common dichotomy is the **sex dichotomy**—the notion that there are but two distinct biological sexes. This, as we will discuss in more detail later in this chapter, is a vision of sex that is deeply rooted in cultural beliefs, especially those beliefs held within Western industrialized nations such as the United States (see Messerschmidt, 2006). These dichotomies serve to limit our understanding of the full complexity of gender as a lived experience and social science construct.

For instance, the gender/sex dichotomy tends to ignore the very real and important links between biological sex characteristics and socially ascribed aspects of gender. In addition, this dichotomy tends to lump together all of the socially ascribed aspects of gender into one broad category. Finally, this dichotomy does not explicitly acknowledge those aspects of gender that are experienced as part of an individual's interior awareness.

Similarly, the sex dichotomy also limits our understanding of the full complexity of gender. This sex dichotomy tends to ignore the influence of culture on our understanding of biological processes. As we will explore, different cultures place different emphases on biology in the determination of gender. While biological characteristics may play a significant role in the gendering of individuals in one culture, they may play a much less significant role in others. If these cultural influences are ignored—which is often the case when we perceive a strict sex dichotomy—we lose the ability to fully address the complexity of gender as a lived experience and social science construct. The model presented in this chapter attempts to address these gender dichotomies through the application of Integral Theory (Wilber, 2000a; 2000b; 2000c; 2001).

The Four Dimensions of Gender

According to Wilber's interpretations of Integral Theory, all human phenomena, including gender, have four distinct, yet interrelated, dimensions. These four dimensions are the interior individual, interior collective, the exterior individual, and exterior collective (see Wilber, 2000a; 2000b; 2000c; 2001). Each of these dimensions relates to a distinct, yet interrelated, aspect of human experience. The **interior individual dimension** corresponds to an individual's subjective experience. Similarly, the **interior collective dimension** corresponds to inter-subjective experience or the shared meaning among a particular group of people (i.e., culture). The **exterior individual dimension** corresponds to objective aspects such as biology and physiology. Finally, the **exterior collective dimension** corresponds to inter-objective aspects such as the functional fit of parts within a social system.

When Integral Theory is applied to the study of gender, a more nuanced understanding of its complexity emerges (see Figure 1). By drawing on research

Figure 1: The Four Dimensions of Gender

Interior Individual Dimension	Exterior Individual Dimension
gender-identity	**sex**
The aspects of gender which are experienced within an individual's own psyche	Biological, physiological, and anatomical traits associated with gendered-beings
Interior Collective Dimension	Exterior Collective Dimension
gender-ideologies	**gender-roles**
Culturally shared beliefs about gendered beings within a given society	Behaviors or activities performed by gendered-beings in a given society which have become institutionalized within various social systems

and theory from a variety of disciplines, we not only gain a more complete understanding of gender but also begin to find ways to communicate that understanding across disciplinary boundaries. Finally, we also begin to find ways to address the complex relationships between people's experiences of gender and their involvement in crime processing as offenders, victims, and employees. Each of the four fundamental dimensions from Integral Theory is discussed here in more detail. This will be followed by a brief discussion of the benefits of taking all four of these dimensions into consideration simultaneously.

The Interior Individual Dimension of Gender: Gender-Identity

Researchers and theorists concerned with the interior individual dimension of gender include those interested in studying how individuals perceive themselves and others as gendered-beings. Perceptions of the self as a gendered-being are sometimes referred to as part of an individual's *gender-identity*. Mealey (2000) defines gender-identity as "one's personal sense of one's own gender, which may or may not correspond to one's sex or to the perceptions of others" (p. 466). A number of theoretical perspectives have been developed to help explain gender-identity development.

Psychoanalytic Theory

Beginning with Sigmund Freud, **the psychoanalytic approach** was one of the earliest attempts at understanding the process of gender-identity formation (Martin, Mutchnick, & Austin, 1990; Rogers & Rogers, 2001). Freud's theory was one of the first investigations of the relationship between gender and psychological development. Freud's theory consists of five distinct developmental stages: oral; anal; phallic; latency; and genital (Rogers & Rogers, 2001). Each of these developmental stages is linked to a particular target of sensual pleasure. According to Freudian psychoanalytic theory, the phallic stage represents the most important stage of gender-identity formation, because it is at this stage that an individual is confronted with very real and tangible differences between biological females and males (i.e., genitalia) (Rogers & Rogers, 2001).

Because Freud's theory was based on the identification of biological sex-differences, he believed that although females and males follow the same developmental path (i.e., moving through the same five stages), they do not necessarily experience each stage in exactly the same manner. In this sense, Freudian psychoanalytic approaches are androcentric (i.e., male centered), contending that boys are more capable of forming a strong gender-identity than girls (see Deutsch, 1944; Erikson, 1968; Stockard & Johnson, 1980). The foundation for such a finding was the emphasis that Freud placed on the phallic stage and his notion of penis envy.

Freud's explicit androcentric analysis of gender-identity formation led to modifications of his original theory. For instance, some psychoanalytic theorists place more emphasis on the pre-phallic stages of development, suggesting that an individual's original orientation is developed during the oral stage, which is marked by the relationship between the child and mother (the sole source of sustenance and therefore sensual pleasure) (Chodorow, 1978; Stockard & Johnson, 1980). Still others argue, as opposed to being a direct reaction to the presence or absence of a penis (i.e., penis envy among girls), that the phallic stage results in the need for both females and males (not just males) to establish independence from the mother (Stockard & Johnson, 1980). Therefore, both females and males go through a very similar process, which is spawned by a drive for independence from and love for the mother.

Although limited due to its overreliance on biological characteristics and its initial androcentrism, the psychoanalytic approach offers four important contributions to our understanding of gender-identity formation. First, the psychoanalytic approach introduced us to the importance of the interior aspects of human existence (i.e., conscious and unconscious thought). Second, the psychoanalytic approach provided an initial framework for understanding the relationship between the psyche and external stimuli (i.e., parent-child relationships). Next, the psychoanalytic approach offered a link (although exaggerated) between the biological (i.e., genitalia) and psychological (gender-identity formation) aspects of gender. Finally, this approach introduced the stage-like nature of gender-identity development.

Social Learning Theory

Social learning theorists argue that the actual mechanisms for learning are the same for both females and males, and that the learning of gender-related information or behaviors is the same as the learning of any other behaviors. Therefore, while the behaviors that each sex displays may be different, the process by which they learn those behaviors is the same. Correspondingly, while gender-identities may differ from individual to individual, the process through which those identities are formed remains constant.

That process includes exposure to both female and male models. All children, therefore, observe and learn gender-related behaviors associated with both sexes (Brannon, 2002; Mischel, 1975). The differences, therefore, are not in the learning, but in the performance or frequency of performance of gender-related behaviors, which are impacted by reinforcement and/or punishment (Mischel, 1975). All sorts of external models influence the learning of "gender-appropriate" behaviors (e.g., the media, parents, peers, teachers). Through the observation of these models in different settings, children learn which behaviors are appropriate for their sex (Brannon, 2002).

The **social learning approach** to gender-identity formation offers a framework in which an individual's social environment has an important impact on their formation of a clear gender-identity. The incorporation of external environmental factors within the social learning approach is in stark contrast to the psychoanalytic approach, which places more emphasis on the internal experiences of individuals and their physical characteristics.

Cognitive Development Theory

So far we have presented two distinct and often competing theoretical approaches to explaining gender-identity formation. In contrast, the **cognitive development approach** was formulated as an attempt to combine the influences of socialization (learning theory) with the internal aspects of human cognition (psychoanalytic theory). Specifically, "… cognitive approaches to gender development involve the underlying premise that whatever information there is in the social world can only have an impact on behavior if there is a certain level of understanding present" (Archer & Lloyd, 2002, p. 70). In addition to attempting to combine aspects of both psychoanalytic and learning theories, cognitive development theorists argue for a more refined stage-based model of gender-identity formation.

One example is Lawrence Kohlberg's (1975) theoretical approach, in which both physical and social factors influence gender-identity development through sequential stages. Kohlberg (1975) suggests that the process of forming a gender-identity involves movement from a somewhat arbitrary labeling of objects, to self-labeling, to the labeling of others, to the adoption of a concrete and unchangeable gender-identity (see Brannon, 2002; Rogers & Rogers, 2001). While the contributions of Kohlberg's theoretical approach are certainly worthwhile and noteworthy, there is at least one major criticism that has been levied against it. Specifically, Kohlberg's theory has been criticized for being androcentric, because it is based on the male experience and tested using male-only samples. In response to the androcentric nature of Kohlberg's approach, Gilligan (1993) applied cognitive development theory to women's gender-identity formation.

Among Gilligan's (1993) findings was the notion that females and males are speaking with "a different voice" in terms of the developmental process. More precisely, Gilligan (1993) states that, "… male and female voices typically speak of the importance of different truths, the former of the role of separation as it defines and empowers the self [ethic of rights], the latter of the ongoing process of attachment that creates and sustains the human community [ethic of care]" (p. 156).

Gilligan (1993) argues that the ethic of care flows along the same general progression as the ethic of rights; however, the ethic of care involves the relationship or interplay between the self and others as opposed to the male path (i.e., the ethic of rights), which is marked by the separation of self from others. In addition, Gilligan (1993) argued that because our understanding of the development of a clear gender-identity is based on the male experience, theorists have continued to elevate the male experience and consider that experience as "normal" development. This, according to Gilligan (1993), leads to female development being relegated to an inferior position, in turn, forcing us to consider females' experiences with development as somewhat less successful or appropriate than the experiences of males.

Gender-Schema Theory

Gender-schema theory attempts to offer an explanation as to why gender plays such a central role in an individual's identity formation. Bem (1981) describes a schema as "… a cognitive structure, a network of associations that organizes and guides an individual's perception" (p. 355). Bem (1981) suggests that during the early developmental stages, children are learning "the particular behaviors and attributes that are to be linked with sex" (p. 354). Thus, as individuals interact with others in society they are generally sex-typed in terms of femininity and masculinity based solely on their external biological makeup. This sex typing leads individuals to form a gender-schema. In other words, as individuals begin to identify with the sex-type that is socially proscribed to them (i.e., feminine or masculine), they will form a gender-schema that will allow them to process information they receive easier, through the lens of that specific sex-type. As a gender-schema is created, it is informed by sex-type specific traits and is then assimilated into the gender-identity of the individual.

Within gender-schema theory the emphasis placed on biological factors is primarily based in the cultural/social belief that these differences transfer to other nonbiological sex differences (Bem, 1981). Therefore, instead of individuals recognizing genital differences and then using them as a basis for personal identity formation, the gender-schema approach suggests that society exaggerates the importance of genital differences (and other relatively unimportant biological differences). The individual internalizes this exaggeration during the early stages of the developmental process. As a result of the internalization of these socially proscribed gender differences, individuals begin to adopt a specific gender-schema. This gender-schema is usually formulated within the context of feminine or masculine attributes, which are intimately linked (at least in the view of some cultures) to biological sex (i.e., female or male).

At this point, an individual begins to organize their entire existence within the context of their gender-schema. This allows the individual to rapidly assimilate and organize new information, by only paying attention to that information which fits within their specific gender-schema (see Levy & Boston, 1994). This leads to individuals ignoring (at least cognitively) knowledge, information, attributes, and/or phenomena that do not fall within the context of their gender-schema. Finally, this will limit the range of behaviors and attributes that an individual will likely choose during their lifespan.

The Interior Collective Dimension of Gender: Gender-Ideologies

Researchers concerned with the interior collective dimension of gender are interested in the meaning that a particular group shares regarding gendered-beings. This could also be described as shared beliefs about the value, characteristics, and traits associated with gendered-beings. These shared beliefs are extremely important in any culture because, as Sanday (1981) points out, they "help men and women orient themselves as male and female to each other, to the world around them, and to the growing boys and girls whose behavior they must shape to a commonly accepted mold" (p. 3). In the model presented in this chapter, the shared beliefs regarding gendered-beings will be referred to as **gender-ideologies**.

Gender-ideologies are intimately linked to origin myths and have serious implications for the relative valuation of gendered-beings within every culture. For instance, some cultures operate with a belief in a common ancestor that is neither female nor male, but "a single, dual gendered or ambiguously gendered being, or an indissoluble pair" (Joyce, 2004, p. 317). The belief in a common ancestor who possesses such characteristics makes it necessary to not only glorify and nurture the female/feminine self, but also the male/masculine self.

For example, some Native American cultures have a long history of a third gender/sex category that combines the attributes of both females and males, or as Brannon (2002) puts it, "individuals who ... blend masculine and feminine roles" (p. 73). These individuals, identified as **Berdaches** (see Brannon, 2002; Lorber, 1994) or *Two-Spirits* (see Bonvillain, 1998), often perform ritual or ceremonial duties. Since the collective beliefs within these Native American cultures support the notion of a common, undifferentiated ancestor, individuals who identify with this third category do not lose prestige for stepping outside the bounds of the female/male, man/woman dichotomy. In fact, in many instances, these individuals are afforded increased prominence and power within a given tribe (Bonvillain, 1998).

Constructions of third, fourth, and fifth genders are also evident in other cultures as well. Andaya (2004) suggests that similar patterns are apparent in the Philippines, where some groups "accorded the same ritual prominence to individuals who combined male and female elements" (p. 328). In some African cultures, similar beliefs about the origin of human existence and the importance of the necessity to "combine male with female elements to ensure that the world worked as it was designed to" also exist (Kent, 2004, p. 92). Similarly, both the **Xanith** in Oman (Archer & Lloyd, 2002; Lorber, 1994) and the **Hijras** in India (Lorber, 1994) are examples of third gender categories. These categories are associated with males who perform duties outside of the context of the normalized male role (e.g., prostitution), as opposed to biological sex characteristics.

In cultures where distinctly gendered deity figures develop, differences in the relative value of men and women often follow. For instance, in some cultures female and male deities are associated with different abilities or experiences. Female deities have been associated with the earth, agriculture, and creation from within (Andaya, 2004; Sanday, 1981; Stockard & Johnson, 1980). Male deities, on the other hand, have been associated with the sky, animals (and hunting), and creation through outside forces (Sanday, 1981). As such, when cultures where dual deities exist are combined with social systems in which value is placed on agriculture, females are often valued to a greater extent than males. The opposite is also true when the combination of culture and social systems works to place greater emphasis on hunting animals and therefore greater value on the male deity and males in general.

As these examples suggest, there is a huge variety of gender-ideologies both within and across cultures. Modern, Western cultures also emphasize a particular set of gender-ideologies. For instance, the current feminine ideology in modern Western cultures is often marked by notions of piety, purity, submissiveness, domesticity, emotionality, obedience, chastity, sensitivity, passivity, and dependence (Brannon, 2002; Clements, 2004; Kollmann, 2004; Sowerwine & Grimshaw, 2004; Valenze, 2004). On the other hand, the masculine ideology is often marked by notions of rationality, intelligence, honesty, courage, strength, and diligence (Brannon, 2002; Clements, 2004). The major distinction, however, is that gender-ideologies within modern Western cultures are viewed as biologically driven. They are therefore perceived as scientific absolutes, which are not impacted by changing cultural viewpoints (Kent, 2004). As we will see in the next section, this focus on biological determinism and the sex dichotomy does not seem to be supported by the relevant research.

The Exterior Individual Dimension of Gender: Sex

The exterior individual dimension of gender refers to the biological, physiological, and anatomical characteristics associated with gender, also referred to as *sex*. We will begin with an overview of how **sex development** generally progresses. This is followed by a discussion of divergences and how they influence our understanding of sex as a biological given.

Research suggests that at its earliest stages of development, the embryo is only sexed in terms of chromosomes, not physical characteristics, and all eggs contain the potential to develop either "female" or "male" physical characteristics (Mealey, 2000), so at six weeks, XX and XY embryos are identical (Brannon, 2002). Interestingly, and contrary to cultural perceptions of the relative strength of the sexes, "male" embryos are more susceptible to trauma and complications (Hutt, 1975; Mealey, 2000).

At roughly seven weeks post-fertilization, the fetal gonad (sex organ) begins to develop. The development of the fetal gonad is determined by the presence or absence of the male chromosome (Y) (Rogers & Rogers, 2001). Once the initial development of the gonad begins, fetal hormones start to impact the development of sex characteristics. The sex hormones are divided into androgens and estrogens. In males (XY), the presence of testosterone (an androgen) and of müllerian inhibiting substance (MIS) causes the development of external male genitalia and the regression of female genitalia, respectively. Interestingly, although each sex develops either female or male external and internal genitalia, each sex also contains the remnants of the other sex's initial internal genitalia.

At roughly 16 weeks, the formation of external genitalia is completed. These external genitalia have a significant influence on our sex typing of individuals throughout the life course. As Messerschmidt (2006) suggests, however, the choice to concentrate almost exclusively on a small range of anatomical characteristics in our assignment of sex is deeply rooted in cultural beliefs and varies from one society to another.

Sometime around the end of the first and beginning of the second trimester, sex differences are found in the organization of the hypothalamus. The hypothalamus controls the pituitary gland, which controls the hormone secretion of all other glands in the body through the production of tropic hormones (Brannon, 2002). Differences in the organization of the hypothalamus have been linked to cyclical production of female hormones as well as some aspects of psychological functioning among both males and females.

In addition, sex differences in the structure of the brain appear during the neonatal period (first month after birth) and beyond. For instance, brain lateralization shows some differences based on sex. Lateralization refers to situations where "the left and right hemispheres are each specialized for different functions" (Brannon, 2002, p. 54). While females use both the left and right hemispheres simultaneously for certain abilities (e.g., language and spatial), males use each hemisphere for specific abilities (i.e., right hemisphere for spatial and left hemisphere for language). It is important to note, however, that the evidence for sex-based differences in brain lateralization is weak, and it has not been shown to directly impact either sex's ability to perform specific tasks (Brannon, 2002).

Another area where sex-based differences in brain structure have been found is in the "Sexually Dimorphic Nucleus" in the hypothalamus (Brannon, 2002). Unlike the difference in brain lateralization, this difference actually shows a relatively strong link to sex. This area of the brain is larger in males, a difference that begins to occur somewhere between birth and two to four years of age. Researchers believe that the major influences on this area of the brain are testosterone and estrogen. However, they are still unclear as to the actual impact that this part of the brain has on individuals, with some suggesting a link to sexual behavior and/or gender-identity (Brannon, 2002). Although there do seem to be general biological differences between females and males in terms of brain structure, research suggests that these physical differences do not necessarily create clear distinctions between the sexes in terms of specific abilities, psychological functioning, or behaviors.

Later in life, puberty corresponds with an increased secretion of specific sex hormones. The increased secretion of these hormones initiates the production of sperm (spermarche) in males or ovulation and menstrual cycling (menarche) in females. There is some variation in the time period when individuals begin to experience changes that are associated with puberty. On average, males in the United States reach spermarche at roughly 13.5 years of age, while females reach menarche at roughly 12.5 years of age (Mealey, 2000). The differing amounts of hormones secreted during puberty in females and males (i.e., estrogens and androgens) create differences in body types and some body functions. The disproportionate increases in androgens experienced by boys compared to girls leads to less body fat, higher body weight, more muscle mass, a higher metabolic rate, and an increased metabolism (Rogers & Rogers, 2001). As with many other sex-differences, however, these differences are recognized as average differences between females and males, not specific to any one individual female or male body.

Historically, the research on adult sexual differentiation has been limited (Steuer & Jarvik, 1981). Even the research that has been conducted has not provided consistent findings in terms of sexual differentiation in adults (Austad, 2001; Steuer & Jarvik, 1981). However, based on some of these limited findings, researchers have suggested that as individuals enter adulthood and continue into old age, the biological differences between females and males begin to diminish (Browne, 2002; Mealey, 2000).

While the discussion above provides a general overview of the more common developmental process, it is important to keep in mind that a number of biological divergences can occur throughout the process of sex-development (e.g., Klinefelter syndrome; Turner syndrome; pseudohermaphroditism; and, 5-α-reductase deficiency). Even our supposedly rigid biological sex-characteristics emerge along a continuum of physiological possibilities; calling into question a distinctly dichotomized view of sex. In other words, what we see as distinct physiological and biological differences between "males" and "females'" is a reflection of our (mis)perception of physical realities and a cultural emphasis on particular biological, physiological, and anatomical characteristics to the exclusion of others.

The Exterior Collective Dimension of Gender: Gender-Roles

Social science scholars are also interested in the study of the exterior collective dimension of gender—**gender-roles**. Those interested in this dimension have predominantly attempted to explain those behaviors or activities that are performed by gendered-beings and have been institutionalized within a given society's social systems. Following this line of reasoning, gender-roles are impacted by the social structure and the structures of particular systems within a society. Two social systems that are intimately related to gender-roles are modes of production and political structures (see Bonvillain, 1998;

Brannon, 2002; Halsall, 2004; Frader, 2004; Sanday, 1981). As changes occur in a society's modes of production, we also see changes in political organization and, consequently, the relative involvement of gendered-beings in both.

There is general agreement that foraging societies present relatively egalitarian gender-role construction (Bonvillain, 1998; Nashat, 2004; Sanday, 1981). As societies begin to develop the ability to farm and produce food through plant cultivation, a shift from foraging to more sedentary and complex horticultural societies begins. In a general sense, horticultural societies are marked by the cultivation of crops, with the assistance of rudimentary hand tools (Stockard & Johnson, 1980). Individuals in horticultural societies are able to produce large amounts of food in a single location. What becomes important in these societies is the relative ability of men and women to exercise power and control over subsistence materials. In societies where women are the major producers of subsistence materials through land cultivation, the value placed on their gender-role increases, and vice versa for societies in which men are the major producers (Schoenbrun, 2004).

Along with the emergence of horticultural societies, we also see an increase in warfare as a means to acquire and maintain land. Researchers have suggested that because of the relative value of women (as producers of children), they are restricted (and likely restrict themselves) from activities that put them in danger of death or serious injury (Stockard & Johnson, 1980). In accord with this gender-role organization, more value is placed on the "male" gender-role, which results in men, at least those who perform this "male" role, being able to wield more power within and between tribes (Halsall, 2004).

The shift from horticulture to agriculture, although certainly fluid in many circumstances, is generally marked by the introduction and extensive use of more complex tools in the cultivation of food (e.g., irrigation, plows, and animals) (Stockard & Johnson, 1980). Perhaps more than any other shift in mode of production, the development of advanced agricultural societies appears to create the greatest changes in gender-role organization (Sanday, 1981; Stearns, 2000; Stockard & Johnson, 1980). As advances in technology allow for increased crop production and, in turn, increased wealth, agricultural societies begin to experience increased birth rates and decreased infant mortality (Stearns, 2000). This creates an atmosphere in which women of childbearing age are relegated to the home, or at least close to the home, while men are free to engage in food production and trading away from the home.

As women are pressed into the private sphere, they are also pulled out of the public sphere, both by men and by the circumstances surrounding the survival of their children, themselves, and their communities. Men, therefore, retain and reinforce their ability to operate within the public sphere, for the benefit of their families as well as the larger social group, and are granted more power and control through the exercise of their now primary gender-roles as providers and political leaders.

Despite the strong shifts in gender-role valuation associated with agricultural societies, Frader (2004) argues that "more than any previous set of economic arrangements, industrial capitalism not only rigidified gender divisions, but also crystallized gender inequalities" (p. 39). It seems, however, that the opposite is true—that as industrialization occurs, the rigidly defined gender-roles previously associated with agricultural societies begin to erode. Through the application of the technological advancements associated with industrialization, modes of production become less tied to biological traits. For instance, both men and women can operate computerized factory machinery.

A more accurate interpretation of Frader's (2004) argument might be that while gender-roles seem to be less rigidly defined in industrial societies, gender-ideologies have yet to catch up. For instance, as both men and women enter the workforce in greater numbers, the relative values placed on their particular jobs differ (Kealey, 2004; Frader, 2004; Lipsett-Rivera, 2004). As women are more likely to enter the public workforce, certain jobs become feminized, while others become masculinized (Lipsett-Rivera, 2004). The jobs that become masculinized also become the jobs which are granted the most social prestige (and often pay), and therefore offer the most power and control.

The rise of industrial nation-states also impacts the development of more rigid gender-ideologies through the process of colonization (Andaya, 2004; Bonvillain, 1998; Frader, 2004; Redding, 2004; Stearns, 2000; Tucker, 2004; Wright, 2004). As large nation-states colonize "less developed" societies, their centralized political structures impose traditional rigidly defined gender-ideologies and gender-roles on individuals and cultures that may not have previously experienced them.

Conclusion

In this chapter, we have outlined a model of gender based in **Integral Theory**. This model suggests that gender can be understood as consisting of four basic dimensions. The interior individual dimension, **gender-identity**, includes the many ways that individuals perceive themselves as gendered-beings. The interior collective dimension, **gender-ideologies**, includes the variety of culturally shared beliefs about the value, characteristics, and traits associated with gendered-beings. The exterior individual dimension, sex, includes the biological, physiological, and anatomical characteristics associated with gender. Finally, the exterior collective dimension, **gender-roles**, includes those behaviors or activities that have been institutionally gendered within a given society's social systems.

As you may have already gathered, however, these paths are not completely distinct or independent. Indeed, each of these dimensions is continuously shaped and reshaped by changes across the other dimensions. One example of this interdependence is in comparing the substance of male gender-roles across societies. In those societies where male gender-roles require increases in physical exertion, the general gap in sex characteristics (e.g., body structure and musculature) between males and females is often exaggerated. In those societies where male gender-roles do not require increases in physical exertion, the general gap in sex characteristics between males and females tends to decrease. In this sense, institutionalized gender-roles have a very real influence on what are usually perceived as inherent sex differences.

Moreover, changes in institutionalized gender-roles can be influenced by shifts in gender-ideologies. As culturally shared beliefs regarding appropriate involvement among women and men in various roles (e.g., policing) become more egalitarian, both women and men begin to engage those roles in more equal numbers. In some instances, this results in the removal of gender considerations from the role altogether. In other instances, and more commonly it seems, this results in a shift in gender-identity among those who perform that role.

For example, females' entry into the field of policing in growing numbers has not resulted in a widespread shift in the masculinized organization and function of the police. Instead, female police officers, just like their male counterparts, adopt and adapt to the masculinized system of policing in order to maintain that role. In this sense, through the institutionalization of gender-roles, systems reinforce particular gender-ideologies and force individuals to adopt particular gender-identities in the performance of those roles.

Of course, the model presented here is not intended to provide all of the answers to the gender puzzle. To the contrary, we hope that this model provides the context in which additional questions may be raised. The real benefit of this model, we argue, is in our ability to view the combined influence of these seemingly distinct dimensions of gender in ways that provide a more complete understanding of individuals' lived experiences. We see this model as an invitation to begin a dialogue about how these dimensions are interrelated. Moreover, we believe the more nuanced picture of gender that emerges through a consideration of all four of these dimensions will better inform our understanding of the relationship between gender and important criminal justice–related issues.

References

Andaya, B. W. (2004). Gender history, southeast Asia, and the "world regions" framework. In T. A. Meade & M. E. Wiesner-Hanks (eds.), *A Companion to Gender History* (pp. 323–342). Malden, MA: Blackwell Publishing.

Archer, J., & Lloyd, B. (2002). *Sex and Gender* (2nd ed.). New York: Cambridge University Press.

Austad, S. N. (2001). The comparative biology of aging. *Annual Review of Gerontology and Geriatrics, 21*, 19–39.

Belknap, J. (2007). *The Invisible Woman: Gender, Crime, and Justice* (3rd ed.).Belmont, CA: Thomson Wadsworth.

Bem, S. L. (1981). Gender schema theory: A cognitive account of sex typing. *Psychological Review, 88*, (4), 354–364.

Bonvillain, N. (1998). *Women and Men: Cultural Constructions of Gender* (2nd ed.). Upper Saddle River, NJ: Prentice Hall.

Brannon, L. (2002). *Gender: Psychological Perspectives* (3rd ed.). Boston: Allyn & Bacon.

Browne, K. R. (2002). *Biology at Work: Rethinking Sexual Equality*. New Brunswick, NJ: Rutgers University Press.

Chodorow, N. (1978). *The Reproduction of Mothering: Psychoanalysis and the Sociology of Gender*. Berkeley: University of California Press.

Clements, B. E. (2004). Continuities amid change: Gender ideas and arrangements in twentieth-century Russia and Eastern Europe. In T. A. Meade & M. E. Wiesner-Hanks (Eds.), *A Companion to Gender History* (pp. 555–567). Malden, MA: Blackwell Publishing.

Deutsch, H. (1944). *The Psychology of Women: A Psychoanalytic Interpretation* (vol. 2: Motherhood). New York: Bantam.

Erikson, E. H. (1968). *Identity: Youth and Crisis*. New York: W. W. Norton & Company.

Esbjörn-Hargens, S. (2006). Integral research: A multi-method approach to investigating phenomena. *Constructivism and the Human Sciences, 11*, 1, 79–107.

Frader, L. L. (2004). Gender and labor in world history. In T. A. Meade & M. E. Wiesner-Hanks (eds.), *A Companion to Gender History* (pp. 26–50). Malden, MA: Blackwell Publishing.

Gilligan, C. (1993). *In a Different Voice: Psychological Theory and Women's Development*. Cambridge, MA: Harvard University Press.

Halsall, P. (2004). Early Western civilization under the sign of gender: Europe and the Mediterranean. In T. A. Meade & M. E. Wiesner-Hanks (eds.), *A Companion to Gender History* (pp. 285–304). Malden, MA: Blackwell Publishing.

Hutt, C. (1975). *Males and Females*. Baltimore: Penguin.

Joyce, R. A. (2004). Gender in the ancient Americas: From earliest villages to European colonization. In T. A. Meade & M. E. Wiesner-Hanks (eds.), *A Companion to Gender History* (pp. 305–320). Malden, MA: Blackwell Publishing.

Kealey, L. (2004). North America from north of the 49th parallel. In T. A. Meade & M. E. Wiesner-Hanks (eds.), *A Companion to Gender History* (pp. 492–510). Malden, MA: Blackwell Publishing.

Kent, S. K. (2004). Gender rules: Law and politics. In T. A. Meade & M. E. Wiesner-Hanks (eds.), *A Companion to Gender History* (pp. 86–109). Malden, MA: Blackwell Publishing.

Kohlberg, L. (1975). A cognitive-developmental analysis of children's sex-role concepts and attitudes. In E. E. Maccoby (ed.), *The Development of Sex Differences* (pp. 56–81). Stanford, CA: Stanford University Press.

Kollmann, N. S. (2004). Self, society, and gender in early modern Russia and eastern Europe. In T. A. Meade & M. E. Wiesner-Hanks (eds.), *A Companion to Gender History* (pp. 358–370). Malden, MA: Blackwell Publishing.

Levy, G. D. & Boston, M. B. (1994). Preschooler's recall of own-sex and other-sex gender scripts. *The Journal of Genetic Psychology, 155,* 3, 369–271.

Lipsett-Rivera, S. (2004). Latin America and the Caribbean. In T. A. Meade & M. E. Wiesner-Hanks (eds.), *A Companion to Gender History* (pp. 477–491). Malden, MA: Blackwell Publishing.

Lorber, J. (1994). *Paradoxes of Gender.* New Haven, CT: Yale University Press.

Martin, R., Mutchnick, R. J., & Austin, W. T. (1990). *Criminological Thought: Pioneers Past and Present.* New York: Macmillan Publishing Company.

Mealey, L. (2000). *Sex Differences: Development and Evolutionary Strategies.* New York: Academic Press.

Messerschmidt, J. W. (2006). Masculinities and crime: Beyond a dualist criminology. In C. M. Renzetti, L. Goodstein, & S. L. Miller (eds.), *Rethinking Gender, Crime, and Justice: Feminist Readings* (pp. 29–43). Los Angeles: Roxbury.

Mischel, W. (1975). A social-learning view of sex differences in behavior. In E. E. Maccoby (ed.), *The Development of Sex Differences* (pp. 56–81). Stanford, CA: Stanford University Press.

Nashat, G. (2004). Women in the Middle East, 8000 BCE to 1700 CE. In T. A. Meade & M. E. Wiesner-Hanks (eds.), *A Companion to Gender History* (pp. 229–248). Malden, MA: Blackwell Publishing.

Redding, S. (2004). Women and gender roles in Africa since 1918: Gender as a determinant of status. In T. A. Meade & M. E. Wiesner-Hanks (eds.), *A Companion to Gender History* (pp. 540–554). Malden, MA: Blackwell Publishing.

Rogers, W. S., & Rogers, R. S. (2001). *The Psychology of Gender and Sexuality: An Introduction.* Philadelphia: Open University Press.

Sanday, P. R. (1981). *Female Power and Male Dominance: On the Origins of Sexual Inequality.* New York: Cambridge University Press.

Schoenbrun, D. (2004). Gendered themes in early African history. In T. A. Meade & M. E. Wiesner-Hanks (eds.), *A Companion to Gender History* (pp. 249–272). Malden, MA: Blackwell Publishing.

Sowerwine, C., & Grimshaw, P. (2004). Equality and difference in the twentieth-century West: North America, Western Europe, Australia, and New Zealand. In T. A. Meade & M. E. Wiesner-Hanks (eds.), *A Companion to Gender History* (pp. 586–610). Malden, MA: Blackwell Publishing.

Stearns, P. N. (2000). *Gender in World History*. New York: Rutledge.

Steuer, J. & Jarvik, L. F. (1981). Cognitive functioning in the elderly: Influence of physical health. In J. G. March (series ed.) & J. L. McGaugh & S. B. Kiesler (vol. eds.), *Aging: Biology and Behavior* (pp. 231–253). New York: Academic Press.

Stockard, J., & Johnson, M. M. (1980). *Sex Roles: Sex Inequality and Sex Role Development*. Englewood Cliffs, NJ: Prentice-Hall.

Tucker, J. (2004). Rescued from obscurity: Contributions and challenged in writing the history of gender in the Middle East and North Africa. In T. A. Meade & M. E. Wiesner-Hanks (eds.), *A Companion to Gender History* (pp. 393–412). Malden, MA: Blackwell Publishing.

Valenze, D. (2004). Gender in the formation of European power, 1750–1914. In T. A. Meade & M. E. Wiesner-Hanks (eds.), *A Companion to Gender History* (pp. 459–576). Malden, MA: Blackwell Publishing.

Wilber, K. (2000a). *Sex, Ecology, Spirituality: The Spirit of Evolution* (2nd ed.). Boston: Shambhala.

Wilber, K. (2000b). *Integral Psychology: Consciousness, Spirit, Psychology, Therapy*. Boston: Shambhala.

Wilber, K. (2000c). *A Brief History of Everything.* Boston: Shambhala.

Wilber, K. (2001). *A Theory of Everything: An Integral Vision for Business, Politics, Science, and Spirituality.* Boston: Shambhala.

Wilber, K. (2006). *Integral Spirituality: A Startling New Role for Religion in the Modern and Postmodern World.* Boston: Integral Books.

Wright, M. (2004). Gender, women, and power in Africa, 1750–1914. In T. A. Meade & M. E. Wiesner-Hanks (eds.), *A Companion to Gender History* (pp. 413–429). Malden, MA: Blackwell Publishing.

Learn More on the Internet:

Integral Institute:
http://www.integralinstitute.org/

Integral Research Institute:
http://www.integralresearchcenter.org/open

1. Why should the four dimensions of gender be taken into consideration when attempting to understand the differences in behavior between males and females?
2. Some cultures have multiple categories for gender/sex, while in the United States we tend to categorize sex and gender into the categories of male or female. What is the purpose of these additional categories? Do you think more categories should be added to the traditional American definition of sex/gender? Why or why not?

Section 2

Race, Gender, and Policing

Chapter Three

Racial Profiling

By Travis Humkey

Introduction

R**acial profiling** can be defined as "the targeting of citizens, based on their race or ethnicity, for additional scrutiny by criminal justice officials" (Gabbidon, Penn, Jordan, & Higgins, 2009). Or as defined by the Department of Justice, "racial profiling is any police-initiated action that relies on the race, ethnicity, or national origin rather than the behavior of an individual or information that leads the police to a particular individual who has been identified as being, or having been, engaged in criminal activity" (Ramirez, McDevitt, and Farrell, 2000, p. 3). More simply, racial profiling is when criminal justice officials, usually in law enforcement, focus attention on an individual or group of individuals simply because of their race.

By whatever definition you choose, racial profiling could take place in a number of different situations. The most publicized of these situations within the criminal justice system (CJS) are police traffic stops, including the dynamic of search and seizure, which addresses **Fourth Amendment** rights. Some would also argue that racial profiling is visible in the racial disparity seen in the prosecution of crime within our court system. Two such examples are the discretionary judgment used by the courts in sentencing, as well as capital punishment. There has also been research concerning the use of racial profiling in the consumer or retail world, as it applies to shoplifting and theft.

History of Racial Profiling

Racial profiling is not a new phenomenon in the U.S. criminal justice system. Beginning in the 1990s, however, the issue began to come into the national spotlight. As far back as the 1960s, the United States National Commission on the Causes and Prevention of Violence determined that "violent crime in the cities stems disproportionately from the ghetto slum where Negros live" (Fridell, p. 37–41). This finding demonstrates the racial tensions that have no doubt played a role in the development of racial profiling as used by police agencies in the United States.

Typically, accusations of racial profiling involve police targeting racial minorities for traffic stops, believing that they are disproportionally involved in criminal activity (Fridell, p. 381). Two lawsuits in particular helped to bring the issue of racial profiling to the attention of the nation: *New Jersey v. Soto* (1996) and ***Wilkins v. Maryland State Police*** (1993). The first lawsuit aimed to suppress evidence discovered as a result of traffic stops that public defenders referred to as an "overrepresentation of blacks among people stopped" along the New Jersey Turnpike (Fridell, p. 381). In *Wilkins*, a public defender and his family were detained along the side of the road while police waited on a drug dog to show up at the scene. This happened after Robert Wilkins refused to let police search his vehicle. Wilkins claimed he and his family were detained due to racial profiling (Fridell, p. 381).

Some in the criminal justice system point to criteria developed during the initial stages of the war on drugs (beginning in the 1980s) used to identify drug couriers. The identifiers were employed by the DEA in training, although the DEA claims to have never used race as a specific identifier in their profiles. Then, beginning in the early 2000s, the terms "racially biased" and "bias-based policing" began to be used to help describe the tensions that have been present in the United States between the police and minority communities even before the 1980s DEA training (Fridell, p. 382). During the discussions that followed, police agencies began to come under pressure to respond to the growing concern from the public and policy makers alike. As a result of this pressure, many police agencies began to standardize methods for data collection and analysis to better identify the racial profiling phenomenon (Fridell, p. 382).

By the mid-2000s many states had passed legislation pertaining to racial profiling. Most included data collection laws and others included laws that addressed training, education, supervision, and accountability and outreach to minority communities (Fridell, Lunney, Diamond, & Kubu, 2001). Many agencies enacted policies addressing when officers may use race or ethnic background when making decisions (Fridell, p. 383). The United States Commission on Civil Rights (2000) laid out recommendations for dealing with racial profiling within the criminal justice system. It called for the passage of legislation targeting the prosecution of those in the law enforcement community who use racial profiling and referred to the issue as its highest priority.

The amount of literature available on the topic of racial profiling predominantly focuses on the phenomenon known as "**driving while black**" or "driving while brown." Many suggestions have been made as to the reasoning and possible solutions to racial profiling when it comes to traffic stops. The main focal point thus far in trying to resolve the problem of racial profiling is to collect and analyze traffic stop data in an attempt to identify the problem. So far, much of the research on "driving while black" has employed similar data collection methods with few variations. This, in turn, has yielded similar findings, as well as similar problems (Kowalski and Lundman, 2007). The most common data collection method used is data as reported by police for traffic stops in certain areas, then to survey African Americans and other minority populations in those same areas, using this second set of data as a benchmark to compare the data gathered from the police reports (Kowalski and Lundman, 2007). Among the growing number of studies on the topic of racial profiling an emerging pattern of disparity has shown that racial minorities are indeed stopped more frequently than their white counterparts (Engel & Canon, 2004; Lange, Johnson, & Vows, 2005; Lundman & Kaufman, 2003; Meehan & Ponder, 2002; Novak, 2004; Rojek, Rosenfeld, & Decker, 2004; Smith & Petrocelli, 2001; Warren, Tomaskovic-Devey, Smith, Zingraff, & Mason, 2006).

One such study was conducted for the San Diego Police Department (Corner, Williams, and Velasco, 2002). It found that there were disparities in the stops made on minority groups. To which, Chief David Bejarano pointed out that even with a clear conclusion that African-American and Hispanic drivers are stopped more often, it does nothing to resolve the problem of racial profiling and the mistrust in police that such a practice creates for those minority communities (Bejarano, 2003, p. 1). A similar study conducted in Cincinnati (Eke, Liu, and Bostaph, 2003) concluded with similar results and a similar problem in that it could not identify a resolution for the disparity.

A 2009 study by Kirk Miller found differences in the number of minorities stopped by local police versus state highway patrolmen. Miller found that highway patrolmen, whose main focus is on highway safety, typically see vehicles moving at faster speeds and may not be able to identify the race of a given driver they stop. Thus, driver infraction was the best predictor for stops made by state troopers or highway patrolmen. On the other hand, due to the nature of their jobs, local police have a tendency to focus on stopping criminal activities. Miller's (2009) findings suggest that, "local police rely upon extralegal factors, including race, more frequently than troopers for nonmoving stops." So with these considerations, Miller found that African American and minority drivers could expect to be stopped more by local than state police for extralegal factors, to include racial profiling (Miller, 2009).

Consumer Racial Profiling

Another form of racial profiling, which functions and has consequences very similar to profiling by criminal justice officials, is identified within the retail world and can be referred to as **consumer racial profiling** (CRP). This aspect of racial profiling highlights the fact that the issue is not unique to traffic stops and court rooms. There are a couple of different specific approaches to racial profiling that take place in the realm of CRP. The first involves racial or ethnic groups not being given equal service by a business, the second is when racial profiling is used to target possible shoplifters or thieves in the retail setting (Jordan, Gabbidon, and Higgins, 2009).

Feagin (1991) was one of the first to research CRP. He interviewed 37 Black middle-class persons from varying American cities. Feagin reported that his respondents often encountered poor service, and were followed as they shopped. Lee (2000) conducted research in a similar fashion in New York and Philadelphia and reached virtually the same outcome as Feagin's (1991) research.

The second way researchers have focused their studies on CRP is to look at the litigation arising from alleged racial discrimination on the part of the retail industry. In 2003 Gabbidon was the first to use this form of analysis. The research showed that clerks were the most likely perpetrators of racial profiling, with security personnel coming in second. Plaintiffs in the 29 cases used for the study were awarded at least a partially favorable finding in 58 percent of the cases.

Jordan, Gabbidon, and Higgins (2009) have also looked at Americans' perception of the practice of CRP and how widespread it is, as well as the views and/or justifications for such practices in the consumer industry. Their research showed that Blacks and Hispanics viewed the use of CRP as more widespread than Whites. Not surprisingly, this practice left them with pessimistic feelings. The research also showed that Blacks were much less likely to feel the use of CRP is justified than both Hispanics and Whites. Interestingly, the 2009 study showed that politics affected the responses as well. More conservative respondents tended to see the use of CRP as being more justifiable than liberal respondents.

In their 2006 study, Birzer and Birzer argue that the U.S. Supreme Court laid a foundation for racially disproportional police traffic stops in their *Whren v. United States* (1996) decision. This case, they point out, establishes that the problem of eliminating racial profiling begins and ends with the courts. In one such example, *Fuchilla v. Layman* (1988), the Court observed that racial profiling seemed to be tolerated—and in some cases even encouraged—by those within the New Jersey State Police (Birzer and Birzer, 2006). In their analysis of *Whren*, Birzer and Birzer (2006) argue that the Court said police could stop any vehicle if they had "probable cause" that the occupants of the vehicle were trafficking weapons or illegal drugs. They argue that because of the amount of data showing the disproportionate number of minorities being stopped by the police, it is essential for the Supreme Court to engineer a test to identify the use of racial profiling by law enforcement.

Central to any court's decision on Fourth Amendment issues, including racial profiling, is whether the judge exhibits the proclivity to adhere to pro-government positions that align with the crime control model approach to criminal justice, or the due process model. The **crime control model** grants considerable discretion to all actors in the justice system, from law enforcement officers, prosecutors, and the courts themselves. Packer (1968) would argue, "the ultimate claim for the Crime Control Model is that the criminal process is a positive guarantor of social freedom" (cited in Pufong & Klumball, 2009). Conversely, the **due process model** argues for strict rule-of-law procedures. To proponents of the due process model, fairness and legality of the criminal justice system is paramount and takes precedence over the greater good or protection of society from criminal activity (Pufong & Klumball, 2009). The due process model very clearly argues for individual rights to come first.

Tillyer and Hartley (2010) also take the position that there is a great deal of discretion used by both the judiciary and law enforcement branches of the criminal justice system. Tillyer and Hartley argue that while sentencing research does historically demonstrate some disparity among racial/ethnic groups, the disparity is reduced when controls such as criminal history are taken into account.

Racial Profiling Litigation

The courts provide a very important service to the criminal justice system in functioning as the interpreter for the laws that policy makers enact. It would stand to reason that the courts have weighed in on issues affecting racial profiling. Indeed, there have been many cases brought to the courts at all levels within the system, some more noteworthy than others. Taking a look at some of these cases will provide for a greater understanding of legal aspects of the issue of racial profiling and how the courts view the subject.

Whren v. United States

Possibly the most significant case regarding the issue of racial profiling in recent years is ***Whren v. United States*** (1996). The case was originally heard in 1995 in Washington, D.C., but was ultimately ruled on by the United States Supreme Court in 1996. In *Whren*, a traffic stop was made by plainclothes police officers patrolling a high drug-trafficking area of Washington, D.C. The stop occurred when police observed an SUV stopped at a stop sign for an inordinate amount of time. They also observed the driver (Brown) looking into the passenger's (Whren) lap, then without signaling, the driver turned and drove off at a high rate of speed. The officers decided to conduct a stop of the vehicle based on probable cause from the traffic violations. After stopping and approaching the vehicle, the officers observed bags of crack cocaine in the passenger's hands. The stop resulted in the arrest of both Brown and Whren (*Whren v. United States*, 1996).

The defendants were convicted in the United States District Court for the District of Columbia. They subsequently appealed the conviction on the grounds that the evidence (bags of crack cocaine) the officers found should have been suppressed due to the fact that the officer had no ability to know that the defendants were involved in drug-related activities and the officers stopped the vehicle based on a pretext assumption. The Appellate Court upheld the conviction of the District Court and the case ended up being appealed to the U.S. Supreme Court (*Whren v. United States*, 1996).

The Supreme Court's decision was written by Justice Scalia and held that: (1) Constitutional reasonableness of traffic stops does not depend on the actual motivations of the individual officers involved; (2) temporary detention of motorist who the police have probable cause to believe has committed civil traffic violation is consistent with Fourth Amendment's prohibition against unreasonable seizures regardless of whether "reasonable officer" would have been motivated to stop the automobile by a desire to enforce the traffic laws; and (3) balancing inherent in Fourth Amendment inquiry does not require court to weigh governmental and individual interests implicated in a traffic stop (*Whren v. United States*, 1996).

In sum, the Supreme Court affirmed the decision of the Court of Appeals and the District of Columbia Circuit Court. They stated that the officer had probable cause to stop the vehicle for traffic violations and that the stop was reasonable under the Fourth Amendment. This was the finding despite the defendants' claims that the officers used the traffic violations as a pretext to investigate further for drugs, based on the defendants' race and the nature of the drug problem in the neighborhood (*Whren v. United States*, 1996).

John Hall (1996) states that the reasonableness of the Fourth Amendment means that a balance must be struck between government interests and individual interests. However, the "objectively reasonable" test is applied so that officers are not left with uncontrolled discretion. To the contrary, Hall argues that the court's decision is not an endorsement for officers to make unconstrained decisions about Fourth Amendment search and seizure practices.

State of New Jersey v. Soto

The *Soto* case was also decided in 1996 and carried huge implications for the law enforcement community regarding racial profiling. It was around this time in the 1990s when the pressure came down from policy makers and courts alike for departments to begin tracking the demographic data of their traffic stops if they had not already begun the process. The *Soto* case involved African American defendants and a motion to suppress evidence on the basis of racial profiling implemented by the New Jersey State Police on at least one section of the New Jersey Turnpike. In this case, the defense put on evidence in the form of traffic and violator surveys conducted by Dr. John Lamberth of Temple University. They followed up with Dr. Joseph B. Kadane of Carnegie Mellon University, who testified that he believed Dr. Lamberth's surveys were conducted appropriately and were reliable for analysis. Dr. Kadane also testified that the surveys showed that Blacks were 4.85 times more likely to be pulled over than Whites on the section of the New Jersey Turnpike from Exit 1 to Exit 3 (*State of New Jersey v. Soto*, 1996).

With this obvious and strong statistical evidence presented, the court granted the defense motions to suppress the evidence, because of the statistically significant discriminator stops. The court ruled that the de facto policy of the New Jersey State Police in targeting Black motorists for investigation and arrest violated both the equal protection and due process clauses of the Constitution, and resulted in the seized evidence being suppressed.

Part of the problem in New Jersey it seems, was the wide berth of discretion given to State Troopers, based in part on the drug interdiction programs run by state law enforcement. In rendering his decision, the Honorable Robert E. Francis noted that, "The eradication of illegal drugs from our State is an obviously worthy goal, but not at the expense of individual rights" (*State of New Jersey v. Soto*, 1996).

United States v. Waldon

In the *Waldon* case, the defendant, Jessie Lee Waldon, was arrested and convicted of bank robbery. Among the motions that Waldon presented at trial was that police used illegal racial profiling against him. In its decision the Appellate Court pointed out that the officer approached the defendant at a bus stop and began a conversation with him and that the contact was consensual and not investigatory in nature. Defining the type of contact, the court said, depends on the officer's behavior and not a subjective suspicion of criminal wrongdoing. The conversation at the bus stop between the officer and Waldon was consensual up to the point that the officer noticed the red dye on Waldon, which of course implicated Waldon in the bank robbery. At no point did the officer act in a coercive fashion, furthering the finding that the contact was not investigatory at the outset (*United States v. Waldon*, 2000).

The judge also determined that the officer did not target Waldon based on racial profiling. The officer simply approached an individual matching the description of the bank robbery suspect, and this description included race along with clothing and general appearance. The decision read, "When determining whom to approach as a suspect of criminal wrongdoing, a police officer may legitimately consider race as a factor if descriptions of the perpetrator known to the officer include race" (*United States v. Waldon*, 1996). In this case the United States Court of Appeals, Sixth Circuit denied Waldon's motions and affirmed the lower court's conviction and sentencing.

Racial Profiling Post September 11th

Yet another form of racial profiling emerged following the devastating attacks on September 11, 2001. A Gallup poll following September 11 showed that a surprising 71% of Black respondents approved of the racial profiling of Arab airline passengers. This is interesting, in that African American populations have always been, and are still, one of the most affected populations due to racial profiling in the United States. What this points out very clearly, is that even when some people believe racial profiling is wrong, they may still see the practice as useful and effective, at least when targeted to other groups.

Another rising theme in the realm of racial profiling is the recent passage of legislation dealing with illegal immigration in the United States. Most notable here is the Arizona bill allowing officers to essentially function as federal immigration officers while using reasonable suspicion to target illegal aliens. Similar bills have either been passed or are currently being considered by legislatures for many states around the country. This is possibly the newest segment in the racial profiling debate. By asking state and local officers to enforce laws against those illegally entering the country, are policy makers actually setting up scenarios for racial profiling to take place? With the Obama administration challenging the Arizona law, it seems the courts will be the deciding factor as they have been so many times before.

Racial Profiling in Immigration Laws

Arizona's 2010 passage of Senate Bill 1070 is perhaps the most controversial new immigration legislation in the country. Senate Bill 1070 states:

> The legislature finds that there is a compelling interest in the co-operative enforcement of federal immigration laws throughout all of Arizona. The legislature declares that the intent of this act is to make attrition through enforcement the public policy of all state and local government agencies in Arizona. The provisions of this act are intended to work together to discourage and deter the unlawful entry and presence of aliens and economic activity by persons unlawfully present in the United States ...

The Arizona bill goes on to state that police officers are to check on the immigration status of all persons, who they have reasonable suspicion to believe, might be illegal aliens. As addressed in a widely read 2010 *Newsweek* article, "Will Arizona's New Immigration Law Lead to Racial Profiling?" Arian Campo-Flores argues that the problem with this scenario occurs when you consider that roughly 30 percent of legitimate Arizona residents are of Latino descent.

Proponents of the Arizona bill say that law enforcement officers could use the legislation to further explore the immigration status of a person they have already approached or pulled over for speeding, for instance. That is, if they have reasonable suspicion that the person is in the country illegally, such as a questionable identification card being presented or struggling with the English language, they may have a legitimate reason to investigate immigration status. Spakovsky (2010) argues that the Arizona law is actually more strictly worded than federal guidelines laid out by the Department of Justice for federal law enforcement agencies. Spakovsky also points out that Arizona took steps toward mitigating the possibility of racial profiling in the new legislation.

To the contrary, Campo-Flores (2010) points out that opponents of the bill argue that with little funding for guidance or training, state and local police departments will struggle to carry out this legislation. Many times the vague interpretation will be left to individual officers' discretion, which could be a recipe for racial profiling events to occur (http://www.thedailybeast.com/newsweek/2010/04/26/will-arizona-s-new-immigration-law-lead-to-racial-profiling.html).

Utah's Senate Bill 81, which went into effect on July 1, 2009, is another such immigration law. Among the bill's provisions is one that allows local sheriffs to cross-deputize their county deputies as federal immigration agents. In fact, "Attorney General Mark Shurtleff says Senate Bill 81, the controversial measure designed to deal with illegal immigration in Utah, 'is convoluted' and filled with 'misunderstanding'" (http://www.ksl.com/?nid=238&sid=6182626). For this reason, many of the local departments in Utah have refused to cross-deputize their law enforcement officers.

More recently, Utah is in the process of trying to pass new immigration legislation, Utah House Bill 497, introduced on March 3, 2011. The bill would require anyone arrested for a felony or class A misdemeanor to prove they are in fact legal U.S. citizens. National Immigration Law Center executive director Marielena Hincapié calls the bill racial profiling and claims it could lead to law enforcement officers demanding that everyone they pull over prove their citizenship, while Utah lawmakers claim that they worked diligently to stay within the parameters of the Constitution, even leaving out the "reasonable suspicion" clause as used in the Arizona Bill.

Possible Solutions to the Problem of Racial Profiling

The issue of racial profiling in emerging immigration law is one that the country is in the midst of addressing. Illegal entry into the United States is a violation of federal law that must be enforced. As one way to address this problem, Higgins, Gabbidon, and Martin (2010) suggest that education programs are needed to educate the public on race relations.

The responsibility to address such issues, however, should lie with the federal government. Requiring state and local law enforcement officers to function outside their usual capacity and adding to this functioning as federal immigration agents is not fair to the officers who face the discretionary decision of whether or not to question a person on their legal status within the United States. This especially becomes an issue when you take into account that in most cases the officers are given no guidance or training on how to identify illegal aliens. Lacking proper training and having little guidance puts officers in the precarious position of using racial profiling to enforce such immigration laws.

Regardless of the reasoning behind racial profiling, the criminal justice community needs to continue to try to identify and understand the causes, so as to prevent both its occurrence and the perception of it happening. Racial/ethnic disparities in the contacts police have within the community can cause mistrust within minority segments of the population and call into question the legitimacy of a police organization (Tyler and Wakslak, 2004). Public opinion polls have consistently demonstrated that a vast majority of Americans are opposed to the practice of racial profiling (Rose, 2002). In addition, the courts have increasingly deemed the use of race (without other suspicious factors) as an unacceptable reason for police to focus enforcement operations on particular groups of people(Wilson, Dunham and Alpert, 2004).

In that vein, many social scientists and criminologists have ventured to ask if the "vast majority" of Americans and the courts find the practice wrong, why does it seem to continue? One possible explanation is that Whites and African Americans (as well as other racial minorities) have fundamental differences in how they view the police and the criminal justice system as a whole. Gabbidon and Greene (2009) noted that while the majority of the public surveyed felt the police did a good job in keeping the community safe, Blacks gave the police lower ratings than Whites, and were more likely to feel the police had treated them with disrespect at some point.

In 2002, Weitzer and Tuch conducted a study to explore the perceptions Blacks and Whites have in regard to racial profiling to include their personal experiences. While both groups agreed the use of racial profiling was wrong, they disagreed on some key elements. The surveys showed that Whites were less likely to believe that Blacks were treated differently by the criminal justice system. Further, Whites also believed that if Blacks are treated differently, it is because Blacks are disproportionately involved in crime, and hence receive a disproportionate treatment from the criminal justice system. This view is also sometimes referred to as "rational discrimination." Such attitudes regarding perceptions of racial profiling can somewhat explain why, even with a seemingly unanimous agreement that the practice is wrong, it still continues.

In like fashion, Hurwitz and Peffley (2010) point out that most Whites see the criminal justice system as "color blind," and therefore assume that the disparities in traffic stops and sentencing are a reflection of a higher rate of criminality for Blacks. Supporting the view that the criminal justice system is "color blind," Taylor and Whitney (1999) point out that data has shown that African Americans commit violent crimes at four to eight times the rate of White American citizens, while the Hispanic rate is three times the White rate. This would support the idea that law enforcement is acting appropriately, and not being discriminatory in their work.

No matter the position you take on the issue, it is especially important to fix the problem of racial profiling and the stigma that accompanies it. Considering that African Americans have the highest rate of criminal victimization in American society, they need to trust the criminal justice system more than other groups. This means that some populations of African Americans are all the more aggravated in that they may be racially profiled at times by the very organizations that should be protecting them (Meares, 1997). This frustration might also lead to an underreporting of crimes by victims who are minorities, because they have a large and growing distrust of law enforcement agencies and the system in total.

References

Alpert, G. P., MacDonald, J. M., & Dunham, R. G. (2005). Police suspicion and discretionary decision making during citizen stops. *Criminology, 43*(2), 407–434.

Bejarano, D. (2003). *Second year of vehicle stop study released* (news release). San Diego: San Diego Police Department.

Birzer, M. L., & Birzer, G. H. (2006). Race matters: A critical look at racial profiling, it's a matter for the courts. *Journal of Criminal Justice, 34*, 643–651.

Brunson, R. K., & Weitzer, R. (2009). Police Relations with Black and White Youths in Different Urban Neighborhoods. *Urban Affairs Review, 44*(6), 858–885.

Campo-Flores, A. (2010, April 26). Will Arizona's new immigration law lead to racial profiling? *Newsweek, Online.* Retrieved October 13, 2011, from http://www.thedailybeast.com/newsweek/2010/04/26/will-arizona-s-new-immigration-law-lead-to-racial-profiling.html

Conder, G., Williams, B., & Velasco, A. (2002). *Vehicle stops in San Diego: 2001.* San Diego: San Diego Police Department.

Eck, J. E., Liu, L., & Bostaph, L. G. (2003). *Police vehicle stops in Cincinnati: July 1–December 31, 2001.* Cincinnati, OH: University of Cincinnati, Division of Criminal Justice.

Ellis, R. (2011, February 3). Immigration bill under scrutiny. *Glasgow Daily Times.* Retrieved October 13, 2011, from http://glasgowdailytimes.com/local/x856147730/Immigration-bill-under-scrutiny

Enforcement of Immigration Laws. AZ SEN. Bill 1070. 49 RS. (2011).

Engel, R. S., & Calnon, J. M. (2004). Examining the influence of drivers' characteristics during traffic stops with police: A national survey. *Justice Quarterly, 21*, 49–90.

Feagin, J. R. (1991). The continuing significance of race: Antidiscrimination in public places. *American Sociological Review, 56*, 101–116.

Gabbidon, S. L. & Greene, H. T. (2009). *Race and Crime* (2nd ed.). Thousand Oaks, CA: Sage.

Gabbidon, S. L., Penn, E. B., Jordan, K. L., & Higgins, G. E. (2009). The influence of race/ethnicity on the perceived prevalence and support for racial profiling at airports. *Criminal Justice Policy Review, 20*(3), 344–358.

Grogger, J., & Ridgeway, G. (2006). Testing for racial profiling in traffic stops from behind the veil of darkness. *Journal of the American Statistical Association, 101*, 878–887.

Hall, J. (1996). Pretext Traffic Stops. *FBI Law Enforcement Bulletin, 65(11)*, 28–34.

Higgins, G. E., Gabbidon, S. L., & Martin, F. (2010). The role of race/ethnicity and race relations on public opinion related to the immigration and crime link. *Journal of Criminal Justice, 38*, 51–56.

Hurwitz, J., & Peffley, M. (2010). And justice for some: Race crime, and punishment in the U.S. criminal justice system. *Canadian Journal of Political Science, 43*(2), 457–479.

Illegal Immigration. UT SEN. Bill 81. GS 2008. (2008).

Ismaili, K. (2010). Surveying the many fronts of the war on immigrants in post-9/11 U.S. society. *Contemporary Justice Review, 13*(1), 71–93.

Jones-Brown, D. D. (2005). Race relations. *Encyclopedia of Law Enforcement* (pp. 395–399). London: Sage.

Jordan, K. L., Gabbidon, S. L., & Higgins, G. E. (2009). Exploring the perceived extent of and citizens' support for consumer racial profiling: Results from a national poll. *Journal of Criminal Justice, 37*, 353–359.

Kowalski, B. R., & Lundman, R. J. (2007). Vehicle stops by police for driving while Black: Common problems and some tentative solutions. *Journal of Criminal Justice, 35*, 165–181.

Lange, J. E., Johnson, M. B., & Voas, R. B. (2005). Testing the racial profiling hypothesis for seemingly disparate traffic stops on the New Jersey Turnpike. *Justice Quarterly, 22*, 193–224.

Lee, J. (2000). The salience of race in everyday life: Black consumers' shopping experiences in Black and White neighborhoods. *Work and Occupations, 27*, 353–376.

Lundman, R. J. & Kaufman, R. L. (2003). Driving while Black: Effects of race, ethnicity, and gender on citizen self-reports of traffic stops and police actions. *Criminology, 41*, 195–220.

Lundman, R. J. (2010). Are police-reported driving while Black data a valid indicator of the race and ethnicity of the traffic law violators police stop? A negative answer with minor qualifications. *Journal of Criminal Justice, 38*, 77–87.

Meares, T. L. (1997). Charting Race and Class Differences toward Drug Legislation and Law Enforcement: Lessons for Federal Criminal Law. *Buffalo Criminal Law Review, 1* (1), 137–174.

Meehan, A. J. & Ponder, M. C. (2002). Race and place: The ecology of racial profiling of African American motorists. *Justice Quarterly, 19*, 399–430.

Miller, K. (2009). Race, driving, and police organization: Modeling moving and non-moving traffic stops with citizen self-reports of driving practices. *Journal of Criminal Justice, 37*, 564–575.

Musgrove, B. (2011, January 7). Immigration enforcement bill heads to Kentucky Senate. *Lexington Herald Leader*. Retrieved October 13, 2011, from http://www.kentucky.com/2011/01/07/1589297/senate-panel-approves-immigration.html

Novak, K. J. (2004). Disparity and racial profiling in traffic enforcement. *Police Quarterly, 7*, 65–96.

Packer, H. L. (1968). *The Limits of the Criminal Sanction.* Stanford, CA: Stanford University Press.

Psarras, C. (2009, April 17). Senate Bill 81 | ksl.com. *Utah News, Sports, Weather and Classifieds | ksl.com.* Retrieved October 13, 2011, from http://www.ksl.com/?nid=238&sid=6182626

Pufong, M. G., & Kluball, C. (2009). Government and individual liberty: The Rehnquist Court's stop and frisk decisions. *Politics & Policy, 37*(6), 1235–1280.

Ramirez, D., McDevitt, J., & Farrell, A. (2000). *A response guide in racial profiling data collection systems: Promising practices and lessons learned.* Washington, DC: U.S. Department of Justice.

Rojek, J., Rosenfeld, R., & Decker, S. (2004). The influence of driver's race on traffic stops in Missouri. *Police Quarterly, 7*, 126–147.

Rose, W. (2002). Crimes of color: Risk, profiling, and the contemporary racialization of social control. *International Journal of Politics, Culture and Society, 16*(2), 179–205.

Smith, M. R. & Petrocelli, M. (2001). Racial profiling? A multivariate analysis of police traffic stop data. *Police Quarterly, 4*, 4–27.

State of New Jersey v. Soto et al., 324 N.J. Super. 66 734 A.2d 350 (NJ. 1996).

Taylor, J. & Whitney, G. (1999). Crime and racial profiling by U.S. police: Is there an empirical basis? *Journal of Social, Political, and Economic Studies, 24(4),* 485–510.

Tillyer, R. & Hartley, R. D. (2010). Driving racial profiling research forward: Learning lessons from sentencing research. *Journal of Criminal Justice, 38*, 657–665.

Tomaskovic-Devey, D., Mason, M., & Zingraff, M. (2004). Looking for the driving while Black phenomenon: Conceptualizing racial profiling bias processes and the associative distributions. *Police Quarterly, 7*, 3–29.

Tyler, T. R. & Wakslak, C. J. (2004). Profiling and the legitimacy of the police: Procedural justice, attributions of motive, and the acceptance of social authority. *Criminology, 42*, 13–42.

United States Commission on Civil Rights. (2000). *Revisiting who is guarding the guardians?: A report on police practices and civil rights in America.* Retrieved October 10, 2011, from http://www.usccr.gov/pubs/guard/main.htm.

United States V. Waldon, 206 F.3d 597 (6th Cir. 2000).

Utah Illegal Immigration Enforcement ACT. UT HR. Bill 497. GS 2011. (2011).

Warren, P. Y. (2010). The continuing significance of race: An analysis across two levels of policing. *Social Science Quarterly, 91*(4), 1026–1042.

Weitzer, R., & Tuch, S. A. (2002). Perceptions of Racial Profiling: Race, Class, and Personal Experience. *Criminology, 40(2).* 435–456.

Whren v. United States, 517 U.S. 806, 116 S. Ct. 1769 (1996).

Willie, C. V., & Edwards, O. L. (1983). Race and Crime. *Encyclopedia of Crime and Justice* (1. [Dr.] ed., pp. 1347–1351). New York: Free Press.

Wilson, G., Dunham, R., & Alpert, G. (2004). Prejudice in police profiling: Assessing an overlooked aspect in prior research. *American Behavioral Scientist, 47,* 896–909.

Wilson, K. (2009). Race, driving, and police organization: Modeling moving and non-moving traffic stops with citizen self-reports of driving practices. *Journal of Criminal Justice, 37,* 564–575.

von Spakovsky, H. A. (2010). The Arizona immigration law: Racial discrimination prohibited. *Legal Memorandum, 58,* 1–7.

Learn More on the Internet:

American Civil Liberties Union on Racial Profiling:
  http://www.aclu.org/racial-justice/racial-profiling
Racial Profiling from the perspective of those who have been profiled:
  http://www.youtube.com/watch?v=OpbNUPrF6II
End Racial Profiling Act:
  http://www.civilrights.org/publications/reports/racial-profiling2011/the-end-of-racial.html

Discussion Questions:

1. Should one's race or ethnicity ever be used by a police officer as a reason to initiate contact with a citizen? Why or why not?
2. Several states have enacted immigration laws that force law enforcement officials to arrest those they suspect to be in the United States illegally. Does this constitute racial profiling? Why or why not?

Chapter Four

Policing and the War on Drugs

By Danielle McDonald

Introduction

I n the United States, the War on Drugs has had a dramatic impact on the criminal justice system. This is particularly true for law enforcement officials who serve on the front line. This chapter will examine the history of the War on Drugs and how it has directly impacted law enforcement as well as inner-city America and people of color. The global impact of the U.S.-led war model also will be examined along with possible alternatives to the current strategy.

President Richard Nixon's War on Drugs

In June 1971, President Richard Nixon declared the United States would engage in a **War on Drugs** in order to fight Public Enemy Number One–drug abuse. During this time, there had been a growing concern over the number of soldiers returning from the Vietnam War addicted to heroin as well as an increase in criminal behavior in the United States, that was directly related to the rise in the number of substance abusers. Drug addiction became a priority and money and man power began to flow into fighting this new war: for example, 2100 federal law enforcement officials were hired, which was an increase of 250% from 1969 (Woolley & Peters, n.d.).

However, it wasn't until 1973 that the War on Drugs became more mainstream with the creation of the **Drug Enforcement Administration** (DEA.). Nixon created the DEA to streamline law enforcement to more efficiently and effectively fight the "… all out, global war on the drug menace" (Woolley & Peters, n.d., para. 2). The overall goal of Nixon's War on Drugs was to provide treatment to addicts and eradicate illicit substances in the United States by focusing law enforcement efforts on drugs being trafficked into the country, and on those who were responsible for selling illicit substances. Although heroin was the main focus in the beginning, by 1975 it became clear that cocaine was the new enemy, when 600 kilograms of Colombian cocaine were seized by Colombian police. This seizure, the largest cocaine seizure to date, led to the Medellin massacre, where 40 people were murdered as retaliation by the drug traffickers in Medellin, Colombia. The massacre demonstrated the growing power of the cocaine drug cartels in Colombia and signaled that there was a new threat. ("Timeline: America's War on Drugs," 2007)

By 1981, the **Medellin Cartel** had formed and was rapidly gaining power as the new alliance began to manufacture and distribute large amounts of Colombian cocaine. The cartel needed a way to get their cocaine into the United States and looked to Panama's leader, **General Manuel Noriega**. General Noriega allowed the cartel to ship their product through Panama into southern Florida. This led to President Ronald Reagan declaring his own war on drugs in October 1982, where the focus was stopping the flow of Colombian cocaine coming into the United States ("Timeline: America's War on Drugs," 2007).

During this same time period, **crack cocaine** was developed and became a popular cheap alternative to **powder cocaine** for the less affluent. The sale of crack cocaine in inner-city neighborhoods led to violence as gangs distributing the drugs fought over turf. The media began to run stories on this violence as well as other sensational stories on infants being born with crack cocaine in their system. Then, in June 1986, basketball sensation **Len Bias** died from a cocaine overdose. Bias, who had hours before signed a contract with the Boston Celtics, was celebrating with friends when he died after consuming a large amount of cocaine. Several news outlets declared that it had been crack cocaine that killed Bias and panic ensued as Americans pondered how crack cocaine could kill a young healthy man such as Bias (Weinreb, n.d.). Crack cocaine then became the new enemy.

President Ronald Reagan's War on Drugs and the Anti-Drug Abuse Act of 1986

The American public was now terrified of crack cocaine and demanded that their politicians react accordingly, and on October 27, 1986, just days before a national election, Congress signed into law the Anti-Drug Abuse Act. This act provided 1.7 billion dollars to fight the War on Drugs, with $97 million being allocated for the construction of new prisons, $200 million for drug education, and $241 million for drug rehabilitation. The act continued to target drugs coming into the United States by increasing taxes on imported goods from countries that did not work with the United States to stop the illegal drug trade from their country. It also targeted high-level drug dealers by making it more difficult for them to launder money through banks and easier for law enforcement to seize their assets once convicted. However, the most notorious part of this act was the reinstatement of **mandatory minimum sentences** for drug offenders. Those who were considered to be high-level dealers, caught possessing 1,000 grams of heroin or 5,000 grams of powder cocaine with the intent to distribute, would be sentenced to a minimum of 10 years in federal prison. Mid-level dealers, or those in possession of 100 grams of heroin or 500 grams of powder cocaine with intent to distribute, would be sentenced to five years in federal prison. A distinction also was made, for the first time, between powder and crack cocaine. Those who were in possession of crack cocaine were sentenced at a rate of 100 times those caught possessing powder cocaine; this was also known as the 100:1 ratio. The **100:1** ratio states that a person caught in possession of 50 grams of powder cocaine would be sentenced to a minimum of 10 years in federal prison and one caught possessing 5 grams of crack cocaine would be sentenced to a minimum of five years in federal prison (Brown, n.d.).

Members of Congress developed the 100:1 ratio based on the belief that crack cocaine was significantly more dangerous than powder cocaine. In 1986, it was believed that crack cocaine was notably more addictive than powder cocaine, and when ingested it was thought to make people behave violently. All one had to do was to look to news stories about violence in the inner city to support these notions and there was support from the black community for the Anti-Drug Abuse Act as well. Half of all black members of Congress voted in 1986 for the Anti-Drug Abuse Act with the hope that these harsh new penalties for this dangerous drug would improve the neighborhoods they saw being destroyed by drug sales and drug addiction. Most members of Congress did not foresee the unintended consequences of these harsh new laws (Brown, n.d.).

Although there was still law enforcement attention directed toward drugs coming into the United States, the new drug on the block, crack cocaine, became a major focus of the War on Drugs. Crack cocaine tended to be sold in an **open-air drug market**, where low-level dealers stood on corners and sold their wares to those who sought them out. These dealers could be found on street corners in American inner-city neighborhoods, and much of the violence that surrounded crack cocaine was over which street gang "owned" which corners (Fryer, Heaton, Levitt, & Murphy, 2006).

The open-air drug market provided law enforcement with an easy mark. Money was put into **surveillance operations** and undercover drug enforcement agents were able to easily watch the drug sales and determine who was selling and buying crack and make arrests within a short period of time. Since many of these low-level crack dealers were in possession of at least 5 grams of crack cocaine, it was easy to build cases against them where they would be sentenced to prison for a minimum of five years. The only problem was that as soon as one person was arrested there was another young poor inner-city youth who was willing to take the gamble and become the next crack dealer on the corner (Fryer, et al., 2006). Young black men in the inner city then became the enemy.

Racial Disparities and the War on Drugs

Those who sold crack cocaine in the inner-city open-air drug markets were primarily black and Hispanic. Once law enforcement began to target low-level inner-city crack cocaine dealers, the number of blacks arrested for crack cocaine dramatically increased—for example, the majority of those sentenced each year to a federal prison for crack cocaine are African American (82.7% in 2007), while only 18% of African Americans report they use crack cocaine (Substance Abuse and Mental Health Services Administration, 2008). Black women also felt the brunt of the War on Drugs as those who were addicted to the drug could be found in possession of and/or selling the minimum amount of crack cocaine needed to enact harsh mandatory minimum sentences. Between 1986 and 1991, the number of black women incarcerated for a drug offense increased by 828% (Mauer & Huling, 1995).

The constant turnaround of young dealers and addicts led to a cycle where one group of young African American men and women would be arrested and sentenced to long prison terms, followed shortly by those who took their place as the dealer on the corner or the addict on the street. Eventually, large segments of young African American men and women were removed from their communities and a significant portion of a generation spent their young adulthood behind bars. This was not the case for whites. Although whites were arrested for drug offenses, they were more likely than African Americans to be arrested for selling or possessing powder cocaine rather than crack cocaine. Powder cocaine drug offenders needed to possess far more powder cocaine to enact mandatory minimum sentences. Therefore, white drug offenders were more likely to be perceived as addicts and receive probation because the amount of cocaine one possessed was below the amount needed to be considered a mid- or high-level dealer. However, black drug dealers only needed to be in possession of a small amount of crack cocaine to trigger a mandatory prison sentence. The disparity in sentencing between crack and powder cocaine led to the U.S. prison system, at the state and federal level, being filled with a majority of people of color. Four out of every five incarcerated drug offenders, for example, are African American (56%) and Hispanic (23%) and the majority (58%) do not have a history of violent offenses or high-level drug activity (King & Mauer, 2002)

The U.S.-Led War on Drugs and Its Global Impact

In order to stop the flow of illegal drugs coming in, the United States needed other countries to buy into the War on Drugs' strategy of stopping illegal drug use through **prohibition** or making the drug illegal and punishing harshly those who use and sell the drug. Over the years, many countries have adopted the prohibition war model. Iran, for example, struggles with opiates crossing its borders from Afghanistan, through Iran, and into Turkey, where the drugs will be distributed to the United States and Europe. Iran has devoted a lot of money and law enforcement efforts into patrolling the border between itself and Afghanistan and has enacted the harshest penalty of all—death for anyone caught trafficking drugs. However, the battle continues between traffickers and law enforcement because the impoverished Afghan is willing to risk his life to drive the opiates to Turkey for the chance to make eight times what the drug is worth in Afghanistan. On May 30, 2011, for example, 300 people imprisoned in Iran were set to be executed for buying, selling, or possessing at least 30 grams of heroin (Roddy, 2011).

Other countries have seen a **displacement effect**, where the war is won in one country only to be moved to another country. In the 1980s, the United States focused a large part of its efforts on powder cocaine coming into this country from Colombia. This increased law enforcement effort led to a number of significant arrests and eventually crippled the Colombian cartels. However, the demand for powder cocaine continued in the United States, and eventually the cocaine market was taken over by **Mexican drug cartels**. In 2006, the president of Mexico, Felipe Calderon, declared his own U.S.-style of war on drugs against the Mexican drug cartels. This **Mexican War on Drugs** has led to the deaths of thousands of Mexicans, including law enforcement, politicians, business owners, journalists, and citizens as well as those involved in the drug trade. The unstable Mexican drug market also has led to violence spilling over into U.S. states that share a border with Mexico ("Mexico under Siege: The Drug War at Our Doorstep," 2011).

Recently, the **Global Commission on Drug Policy** (2011) concluded, "The global war on drugs has failed, with devastating consequences for individuals and societies around the world. Fifty years after the initiation of the UN Single Convention on Narcotic Drugs, and 40 years after President Nixon launched the US government's war on drugs, fundamental reforms in national and global drug control policies are urgently needed" (p. 2). The United Nations estimates of annual drug usage from 1998 to 2008 show drug consumption increased during this time period even though the global war on drugs was in full swing. Specifically, between 1998 and 2008, opiate usage increased by 34.5%, cocaine usage increased by 27%, and cannabis usage increased by 8.5% (Global Commission on Drug Policy, 2011). During the global war on drugs, which has focused on punishment and prohibition, illegal drugs have become more widely available and cheaper, and consumption has increased (Caulkins & Chandler, 2005).

Other Options: LEAP, Legalization, and Decriminalization

Not all involved in law enforcement agree with the tactics of the War on Drugs and with the way the war is being fought. For example, **Law Enforcement against Prohibition**, or LEAP, is a nonprofit organization consisting of law enforcement and other criminal justice professionals from the United States who disagree with the current prohibition war strategy. LEAP advocates the **legalization** of all currently illegal drugs with government control and regulation similar to the way alcohol is currently regulated in the United States (Law Enforcement against Prohibition, n.d.). Other countries, such as the Netherlands, have tried this strategy with marijuana with some success. In the Netherlands, marijuana is regulated very similarly to how alcohol is regulated in the United States. One can only purchase marijuana in small amounts from coffee shops. Coffee shops also sell beverages such as sodas or coffee, but do not sell alcohol. Patrons of the coffee shops are allowed to smoke within the shop, but cannot smoke the marijuana in public places such as the street or parks. Marijuana growers and distributors are regulated and taxed by the government. These coffee shops used to be open to anyone over the age of 18. However, concerns over marijuana being trafficked into neighboring countries where it is illegal have prompted the Netherlands to require proof of Dutch citizenship to partake in their coffee shops. Although there is a growing movement within the United States to legalize marijuana, particularly for medicinal purposes, the same support for legalization is not found for harder drugs such as cocaine and heroin (Global Commission on Drug Policy, 2011).

Other countries, such as Portugal, have taken a **decriminalization** approach to all illegal drugs. In Portugal, it is still illegal to possess, buy, or sell drugs such as heroin, marijuana, and cocaine, but law enforcement does not target those in possession of illegal drugs. Many speculated that this would lead to an increase in the use of illegal substances, but after ten years of this policy the Portuguese have concluded that "… removal of criminal penalties, combined with the use of alternative therapeutic responses to people struggling with drug dependence, has reduced the burden of drug law enforcement on the criminal justice system and the overall level of problematic drug use" (Global Commission on Drug Policy, 2011, p. 10).

Other Options: Drug Market
Intervention Initiative

The **Drug Market Intervention Initiative** (DMII) is another strategy gaining popularity among law enforcement in fighting the War on Drugs. The DMII involves actors from the criminal justice system (police, prosecutors, judges, probation, and parole) working with social services and community members to end drug sales in neighborhoods with open-air drug markets. The goal of this program is to dissolve the open-air drug market and reduce the violent crime that is often associated with this type of drug market. First, law enforcement must identify where the open-air drug market is located. This is done through **crime mapping**, which allows law enforcement to identify where the hot zones are located by examining 911 calls, field contacts made by narcotics units, as well as arrest rates for drug crimes, prostitution, and weapons. Once the area has been located, the community, along with police and probation, work together to identify who is selling drugs within the neighborhood and where they live. Next, the police investigate to determine which dealers are still active in the community and if they are a street-level or mid-level dealer and if they have a history of violence or any pending arrests. Those who have outstanding warrants and those who are determined to be a danger to the community are arrested by police immediately. The police then begin to build their case against the nonviolent, typically street-level dealers who are left through undercover operations. While the police are conducting their investigations, the community is coming together to build a united front against the crime and violence that is occurring within their neighborhood. Community leaders are identified and enlisted to get the rest of the community involved (Kennedy & Wong, 2009).

Once the police have built their case against the remaining low-level drug dealers, the district attorney's office, along with the help of law enforcement and community leaders, goes to each drug dealer's house. An unsigned warrant for the dealer's arrest is then presented to illustrate that the police are aware of their illegal actions. The drug dealer and/or their family members are told that the dealer will not be arrested if he/she attends the community notification session, but if they do not attend the meeting they will be arrested the next day (Kennedy & Wong, 2009).

When the drug dealers arrive at the **community notification session**, they are greeted by a room full of community members, law enforcement, and the district attorney. The dealers are asked to take a seat at the front of the room. The district attorney then presents the evidence against each dealer including video and photo surveillance and explains that if they do not participate in the opportunity they are given on this night, they will be facing several years in prison. Next, community members take turns discussing how the dealer's actions have directly impacted their families and their communities and are told emphatically that they will not put up with their illegal behavior any more. Finally, the drug dealers are told that they are an integral part of their community and they want to offer them a chance to go straight and become a productive member of the community. The dealers are offered assistance with social services such as food, clothing, and shelter, counseling, and job training, but are told that if they are caught doing anything illegal they will be arrested and the evidence that has been collected will be used against them. Follow-up sessions are provided for the drug dealers to give continued support and services (Kennedy & Wong, 2009).

The first DMII was conducted in the West End community of High Point, North Carolina. A month prior to the community notification sessions, police were able to make several drug buys from 11 people in 17 different places. A month later, informants were sent to 16 locations and were unable to make one drug purchase. Five years after the intervention, violent crimes have decreased by 57%, and no homicides, rapes, or gun assaults have been reported since the intervention, with gunshot calls to police dropping by more than 50%. "No displacement has been evident. Of the 18 dealers notified in the first two initiatives only four have been arrested for dealing, three in their initial areas and one elsewhere. No other hot spots have emerged; rather, High Point has improved overall after each call-in" (Kennedy & Wong, 2009, p. 17). Another positive outcome is the improved relations between law enforcement and the community. When community members were surveyed and asked what their biggest complaint about the police would be, 30% complimented the police or stated they had no problems. One drawback seems to be that ex drug dealers who did not reoffend have a difficult time reintegrating back into their community. In High Point, for example, only one ex dealer was able to maintain consistent employment (Kennedy & Wong, 2009).

Other Options: Switzerland's Four Pillar Approach

Switzerland, like many European countries, once engaged in a U.S.-style war on drugs. However, they found that this tactic did not decrease their drug addiction or drug trafficking problems and began to look for other ways to eliminate their troubles. In the 1980s, injection drug use soared in Switzerland as heroin became a popular drug of choice. Heroin and injection drug use led to an increase in drug overdoses, crime, and the highest HIV rates in western Europe. First, the Swiss tried a decriminalization approach, where they asked law enforcement not to target drug users who they recognized as addicts with a medical condition, but only the traffickers bringing drugs into Switzerland.

Therefore, it was not legal to use or possess heroin, but heroin users were not targeted by law enforcement, either. This led to large numbers of heroin users, sometimes as many as 1,000 a day, gathering in the park in Zurich to inject heroin. The Swiss citizens were outraged that their public spaces had been taken over by addicts who had nowhere else to go, and through a voter referendum instituted what is known as the Four Pillars (Csete, 2010).

The four pillars model works to eradicate drug trafficking and drug addiction from four vantage points—prevention, treatment, community policing, and harm reduction. Through prevention efforts, the youth were educated about the dangers of heroin and drug abuse with the hopes that the next generation, armed with knowledge, would make better choices. Those who were known addicts were offered placements in treatment programs and were viewed as addicts with a medical condition rather than criminals. The police continued to focus on drug trafficking, and when they encountered someone in possession of heroin who was not viewed to be a trafficker they did not arrest him/her, but instead connected the person to social services. Harm reduction occurred through supervised injection sites, methadone clinics, and prescription heroin. Supervised injection sites resembled medical clinics and reduced harm by providing a safe environment for addicts to inject heroin with access to clean needles and medical staff if an overdose occurs. Treatment staff also is on hand to offer services if one should seek them out. Methadone clinics and prescription heroin are available as options for the small percentage that are unsuccessful with more traditional routes of substance treatment. This model works to reduce the number of new users through prevention and treats those already addicted, which in turn diminishes the demand for the drug and leads to less trafficking and a reduced amount of availability of the drug (Csete, 2010).

The **four pillars model** was first introduced in 1991 and has been quite successful in reducing the number of heroin users—for example, in 1990 there were 850 new heroin users, but by 2002 this number had been reduced to 150. Between 1991 and 2004, drug-related HIV infection declined and drug-related deaths decreased by half, while property crime has been reduced by 90%. Most addicts have sought out treatment, with 70% of injectors in treatment. This model has not always been politically popular, but the Swiss citizens have managed to keep the four pillars model in place by voting it in, initially through a voter referendum and then voting down an attempt to stop the program later on (Csete, 2010).

Summary

Forty years later, the U.S.-led War on Drugs model has not been a success. In the United States and worldwide, illegal drugs such as cocaine, opiates, and marijuana are more potent, cheaper, and easier to access than prior to the start of the war. This war also has had a major impact on communities as large numbers of low-level drug offenders, typically people of color, were removed from their communities. In 1972, prior to the start of the War on Drugs, there were 3,384 drug offenders incarcerated in federal prison and 19,996 in state prisons, but by 2002 there were 63,898 drug offenders incarcerated in federal prison and 252,249 in state prisons (Caulkins & Chandler, 2005).

Recently, society has begun to recognize that powder cocaine is just as addictive as crack cocaine and the violence that was once thought to be associated with the use of crack had more to do with an unstable drug market as gangs battled over turf to sell their drugs. This realization, along with the awareness of the unintended consequences of the War on Drugs on inner-city America—and in particular, African Americans—has led to some changes within the war. In 2010, for example, the **Fair Sentencing Act** was passed. This act abolished the federal mandatory minimum sentence of imprisonment for possession of 5 grams of crack cocaine and reduced the ratio of crack to powder cocaine to 18:1 for other crack cocaine–related mandatory minimum sentences. This is a step in the right direction in reducing the negative impact of the War on Drugs on people of color and the inner city, but more must be done.

There are other options for reducing drug use and trafficking besides the war model, and several that have been shown to be effective in the United States and globally. It is now the time to try a different approach. However, this time around we need to monitor the implementation of the policy more carefully and evaluate the effectiveness of it. These types of policy evaluations will allow for improvement of the policy and for unintended consequences to be addressed immediately, instead of 25 years later.

References

Brown, D. K. (n.d.). Anti-Drug Abuse Act (1986). In *Major Acts of Congress*. Retrieved from http://www.enotes.com/major-acts-congress/anti-drug-abuse-act

Caulkins, J P., & Chandler, S. (2005). Long-run Trends in Incarceration of Drug Offenders in U.S. *Heinz Research, paper 21*. Retrieved from http://repository.cmu.edu/heinzworks/21/

Csete, J. (2010). From the Mountaintops: What the world can learn from drug policy change in Switzerland. *Open Society Foundations*. Retrieved from http://

www.soros.org/initiatives/drugpolicy/articles_publications/publications/csete-mountaintops-20101021

Fryer, R. G., Heaton, P. S., Levitt, S. D., and Murphy, K. M. (2006). Measuring Crack Cocaine and Its Impact. National Bureau of Economic Research, Inc. working papers with number 11318. Retrieved from http://www.economics.harvard.edu/faculty/fryer/files/fhlm_crack_cocaine.pdf

Kennedy, D. M., & Wong, S. (2009). The High Point Drug Market Intervention Strategy. U.S. Department of Justice, Office of Community Oriented Policing Services. Retrieved from http://www.cops.usdoj.gov/files/RIC/Publications/e08097226-HighPoint.pdf

King, R. S., & Mauer, M. (2002). Distorted Priorities: Drug Offenders in State Prisons. *The Sentencing Project*. Retrieved from http://www.sentencingproject.org/doc/publications/dp_distortedpriorities.pdf

Law Enforcement against Prohibition (n.d.). Retrieved from http://www.leap.cc/

Mauer, M., & Huling, T. (1995). Young black Americans and the Criminal Justice System: Five Years Later. The Sentencing Project. Retrieved from http://www.sentencingproject.org/doc/publications/rd_youngblack_5yrslater.pdf

Mexico Under Siege: The Drug War at Our Doorstep (n.d.). In *Los Angeles Times*. Retrieved from http://projects.latimes.com/mexico-drug-war/#/its-a-war

Report of the Global Commission on Drug Policy (2011). Retrieved from http://www.globalcommissionondrugs.org/Report

Roddy, M. (2011, May 30). Iran says to hang 300 drug traffickers—report. *Reuters Africa*.
Retrieved from http://af.reuters.com/article/worldNews/idAFTRE74T1L520110530

Substance Abuse and Mental Health Administration. (2008). 2007 National Survey on Drug Use & Health.

Timeline: America's War on Drugs. (2007). Retrieved from http://www.npr.org/templates/story/story.php?storyId=9252490

Weinreb, M.(n.d.). The Day Innocence Died. Retrieved from http://sports.espn.go.com/espn/eticket/story?page=bias

Woolley, J., & Peters, G. (n.d.). Message to Congress Transmitting Reorganization Plan 2 of 1973 Establishing the Drug Enforcement Administration. *In The American Presidency Project*. Retrieved from http://www.presidency.ucsb.edu/ws/index.php?pid=4159#axzz1W9Yg9Ugm

Learn More on the Internet

Drug Enforcement Administration (DEA):
   http://www.justice.gov/dea/
Law Enforcement against Prohibition:
   http://www.leap.cc/

Mexico under Siege: The Drug War at Our Doorstep:
http://projects.latimes.com/mexico-drug-war/

Discussion Questions

1. Why has the War on Drugs been referred to as a war against people of color and the poor? Is this an accurate statement?
2. Should the United States move toward a drug policy of legalization and/or decriminalization, or should the current prohibition of illegal drugs remain in effect?

SECTION 3

RACE, GENDER, AND THE COURTS

CHAPTER FIVE

Specialty Courts

By Michael Bush

Introduction

The increasing number of special needs offenders in the nation's courtrooms and correctional facilities has led many jurisdictions to create specialty courts for dealing with certain types of offenders or crimes. **Special needs offenders** are those who engage in crime and criminality due to specific reasons, such as drug or alcohol abuse or mental illness. **Specialty courts** deviate from the traditional model used in court proceedings as they provide a non-adversarial environment that focuses on problem solving and treatment rather than incarceration (Tyuse & Linhorst, 2005). As such, specialty courts require more of a consensual approach from judges, prosecutors, defense attorneys, and treatment providers who work together to provide community-based treatment for offenders.

Traditional court procedures have had little effect on special needs offenders as they cycle through courtrooms, jails, and neighborhoods over and over. Consider that nearly one half of inmates in correctional facilities in the United States confess to being under the influence of drugs or alcohol when committing the offense that led to their incarceration, and about 70% to 80% of offenders report using drugs at some point in their lives (Lab, Williams, Holcomb, Burek, King, & Buerger, 2011). Similarly, between 5% and 20% of inmate populations include persons with mental illness (Mental Health Courts, 2006; Lab, et al., 2011).The number of incarcerated offenders with mental illness has led some to consider America's correctional facilities as the new mental health hospitals (Tyuse & Linhorst, 2005).As an example, "it's estimated that more people with major mental illness (schizophrenia, bipolar disorder, or major depression) are detained in Illinois' Cook County Jail than are admitted to all psychiatric hospitals in the state combined" (Mental Health Courts, 2006, p. 4). Furthermore, those offenders who are mentally ill are more likely to be under the influence of drugs or alcohol at the time of their offense than those offenders who are not mentally ill.

Offenders who are classified as having both substance abuse problems and mental health problems are referred to as **dual-disorder offenders** (Lab et al., 2011). Dual-disorder offenders present additional concerns for traditional courtrooms and correctional facilities. These offenders are typically arrested more frequently for less serious offenses and are generally turned away from treatment in traditional psychiatric facilities because of their substance abuse problems. As a result, many jurisdictions have implemented drug courts and mental health courts to deal with the high number of offenders that require specific attention in these areas. The following sections discuss both drug courts and mental health courts.

Drug Courts

An obvious, yet complex, relationship exists between drug abuse and crime, evidenced by the number of drug-involved offenders that have been processed by the criminal justice system in the last 25 years (DeMatteo, 2010). A significant proportion of inmate populations are comprised of first-time or minor drug offenders who were the result of the "War on Drugs" in the 1980s and the corresponding "get tough" movement that led to more punitive sentences for drug offenders. The increased enforcement and punishment of drug offenses resulted in court systems and correctional facilities becoming overwhelmed with substance abuse offenders. The large number of caseloads, and the courts' frustration with their inability to effectively respond to these offenders, revealed a necessity for the criminal justice system to explore alternative measures, which resulted in the creation of drug courts (Fulkerson, 2009; Hora, 2002; Lab et al., 2011; Stinchcomb, 2010; Thompson, Osher, & Tomasini-Joshi, 2007).

Drug courts are designed to provide a treatment-oriented approach for responding to offenders with a history of drug abuse, while also ensuring judicial supervision of offenders, and court-ordered sanctions when necessary (DeMatteo, 2010; King & Pasquarella, 2009). **Drug courts** are community-based programs that use substance abuse treatment along with court supervision and court appearances to assist offenders with completion of their treatment programs. Their specific purpose is to "interrupt the recurring pattern of addiction and criminal behavior, restore the person to a life without drugs and crime, help the addict accept responsibility for his or her actions, restore drug addicts to their families, make society safer, and repair the harm caused by drug addiction" (Fulkerson, 2009, p. 264).

Historical Overview of Drug Courts

Drug courts developed as an alternative to the punishment-oriented model that had evolved from the "get tough" movement toward crime and criminality. Traditional methods of addressing drug use and abuse in the criminal justice system were through a law enforcement approach that resulted in the incarceration of large numbers of people. However, the criminal justice system began to realize in the late 1980s and early 1990s that incarceration alone was largely ineffective for responding to the relationship between drug use and crime. This realization, combined with an increasing acceptance of the medical model toward addiction, led to greater support for court-ordered and court-supervised treatment as an appropriate response to criminal behavior by offenders with substance abuse problems.

The first drug court was established in Miami-Dade County, Florida, in 1989 and would serve as a model for later drug courts ("About the Drug Courts," 2000; Fulkerson, 2009; King & Pasquarella, 2009; Tyuse & Linhorst, 2005). This original court worked with defendants prior to sentencing and incorporated case processing, periodic drug testing, judicial supervision and close monitoring, counseling, access to educational and vocational programs, and incentives for promoting compliance, as well as sanctions for noncompliance. There was no theoretical basis or nationwide support for the creation of the first drug court. Rather, several communities became increasingly upset over the "revolving door" nature of drug use, incarceration, the failures of probation and parole, and the cycling back and forth of low-level drug offenders between local neighborhoods and the criminal justice system (Cosden, Baker, Benki, Patz, Walker, & Sullivan, 2010; Hora, 2002).

The federal government began providing funds for the development of drug courts as a response to their increasing support. The U.S. attorney general distributed federal funds to local jurisdictions through the Violent Crime Control and Law Enforcement Act of 1994. Between 1995 and 1999, this act provided more than 100 million dollars for the development and implementation of drug courts. There were 2,193 fully operational drug courts in the United States and 208 that were planned for operation as of February 2011 (NCJRS, 2011). Some drug courts have been modified to address the unique problems faced by families, women, juveniles, and Native Americans. As the number and type of drug courts increased over the years, it became necessary to define the fundamental principles needed to ensure their effectiveness.

Conceptual Foundation and
Theoretical Model

Treatment is the foundational component of the drug court model. Drug courts are non-adjudicatory in nature and seek diversion for offenders through rigorous substance abuse treatment programs rather than prosecution (Fulkerson, 2009; Stinchcomb, 2010). In contrast to the traditional approach of arresting and punishing substance abuse offenders, drug courts provide access to a range of treatment services while offenders' drug-related behavior is monitored through frequent testing. It is important to note that treatment may vary in terms of quality, quantity, and type of approach, as not all jurisdictions will have equal access to the same resources.

Drug courts embrace the disease model of addiction, which recognizes that offenders are suffering from a chronic condition and are likely to experience some relapses into their substance abusing behaviors (Shaffer, Hartman, & Listwan, 2009). These treatment failures are expected, and consequences exist for those who violate these conditions, but participants are typically not removed from the program. Rather than remove an offender from the program, it is important for judges to determine whether an individual is making overall progress despite the inevitable relapses that typically occur. It is especially important for the judge to accept the disease model as the judge is the team leader, and his or her attitude will likely set the tone for others who are involved (King & Pasquarella, 2009).

Prosecutors also must adopt very different roles in drug courts than they do in traditional courts (Fulkerson, 2009; Hora, 2002; Stinchcomb, 2010). The prosecutor must compromise the usual approach of determining whether or not he or she can obtain a conviction. Instead, the prosecutor must decide whether or not the defendant could benefit from the drug court program. The

Table 1: The Ten Key Components of Drug Courts

1. Drug courts integrate alcohol and other drug treatment services with justice system case processing.
2. Using a non-adversarial approach, prosecution and defense counsels promote public safety while protecting participants' due process rights.
3. Eligible participants are identified early and promptly placed in the drug court program.
4. Drug courts provide access to a continuum of alcohol, drug, and other related treatment and rehabilitation services.
5. Abstinence is monitored by frequent alcohol and other drug testing.
6. A coordinated strategy governs drug court responses to participants' compliance.
7. Ongoing judicial interaction with each drug court participant is essential.
8. Monitoring and evaluation measure the achievement of program goals and gauge effectiveness.
9. Continuing interdisciplinary education promotes effective drug court planning, implementation, and operations.
10. Forging partnerships among drug courts, public agencies, and community-based organizations generates local support and enhances drug court effectiveness.

Source: Hora, P. F. (2002). A dozen years of drug treatment courts: Uncovering our theoretical foundation and the construction of a mainstream paradigm.

role of the defense attorney in the drug treatment court model is also very different than in the traditional court model (Fulkerson, 2009; Hora, 2002; Stinchcomb, 2010). In the traditional model, the defense counsel seeks the most favorable disposition for his or her clients, which is usually an attempt to avoid or reduce possible sanctions. In drug courts, defense counsel must assist with the screening process of offenders and help determine whether or not they are eligible for treatment programs. In other words, the defense counsel functions to keep the defendant in the system, as opposed to working to keep him or her out of the system.

The persons and agencies providing treatment must also assume different roles in the drug court model than they normally would (Fulkerson, 2009; Hora, 2002; Stinchcomb, 2010). Treatment providers maintain a presence in all court proceedings, which allows for immediate access to treatment information so the court may apply rewards for those successfully progressing through the program and sanctions for those who are not. Overall, a coordinated effort is required of judges, prosecutors, defense counsel, case managers, and various treatment providers in order to create an effective treatment program.

Theoretically, drug courts reflect the growing initiative of therapeutic jurisprudence (Fulkerson, 2009; Stinchcomb, 2010; Vrecko, 2009). **Therapeutic jurisprudence** is a legal concept that originated in mental health law and has since expanded into the realms of health care, domestic violence, corrections, criminal justice, and contractual law (Fulkerson, 2009). Therapeutic jurisprudence is described as having a problem-solving focus and as being outcome-oriented. The emphasis on outcomes is one feature of drug courts that sets them apart from traditional models of jurisprudence. Traditional models are typically more concerned with application or interpretation of law and legal principle, while therapeutic jurisprudence is more concerned with the consequences or outcomes of a legal decision. Since courtrooms are not equipped as drug treatment centers, this type of approach requires a cooperative effort from various professionals and agencies that are collectively seeking the most effective therapeutic outcomes for offenders.

The Ten Key Components of Drug Courts

The Ten Key Components were created by judges, prosecutors, defense attorneys, treatment providers, and various court administrators and are intended to reduce recidivism of drug-related crimes through treatment and the promotion of recovery and abstinence in offenders (Hora, 2002). It is recommended that drug courts implement these ten key components in order to ensure effectiveness. The first component recommends that treatment personnel— the judge, prosecutor, defense counsel, pretrial services, probation or other corrections personnel, police, and treatment service providers—ensure the defendant understands exactly what is required for successful completion of the program. The second component emphasizes the non-adversarial approach of the court, which requires collaboration from the various treatment personnel mentioned above. Although the participant's recovery is the primary focus, this component also mentions the goal of public safety, which is still a concern of the courts. Component three indicates the need for early identification and quick placement of eligible participants, which also requires teamwork from the various treatment personnel in the drug court model. Most courts require immediate enrollment in treatment services once a defendant is determined to be eligible.

Key Components four through six refer to alcohol and drug treatment (Hora, 2002). Component number four recognizes the need to provide a range of treatment options to eligible participants as well as continued treatment based on their individualized needs. Services offered to participants will vary depending on treatment resources available, but generally include mental health evaluations, communicable disease testing and education, clean and sober housing referrals, employment training and assistance, vocational training, educational assessments, and counseling. The fifth component suggests frequent testing for alcohol and other drug use. Frequent testing is conducted to measure treatment effectiveness and for adjustments to be made to treatment plans rather than for the purpose of "catching" someone and punishing him or her. Drug courts recognize that addiction is difficult and relapsing is common, and that it may take participants several attempts before significant progress is seen in their treatment. Component six refers to courts using a range of responses for both compliance and noncompliance. This component reinforces the goal of treatment, and responses may range from praise, respect, and encouragement from the court to threats of program removal or shock incarceration. Shock incarceration is a sanction that generally includes an intense, but relatively short, period of incarceration that emphasizes military-style discipline, obedience to orders, and a highly rigid structure. It is usually followed by a period of community supervision of the offender (Clark, Aziz, & MacKenzie, 1994).

The seventh component refers to judicial interaction between the judge and participants (Hora, 2002). One of the unique aspects of the drug court model is the frequency with which judges interact with participants. The judge's role is considered a continuing partnership with a participant that extends beyond the adjudication stage, and is less formalistic than in traditional courtrooms. Frequent and meaningful interaction between judges and participants tends to positively influence participants of drug court programs. Thus, it appears that a judge may play an important role in determining drug court outcomes.

The final three components refer to organizational mechanisms that are necessary for drug courts to be effective (Hora, 2002). The eighth component recommends continual evaluation of drug court programs. Evaluation allows for the promotion of the most effective outcomes for participants in drug court programs, and also serves to further legitimize the continued use of drug courts for offenders with substance abuse problems. Component nine refers to continued education about drug court operations, which is intended to increase effectiveness for both procedures and outcomes. The tenth and final component refers to the integral nature of drug courts and emphasizes the importance of building relationships with various agencies so as to increase participant opportunities and performance.

Target Population & Program Components

Offenders who are eligible for participation in drug court programs differ from jurisdiction to jurisdiction; however, defendants are generally those who are charged with a nonviolent drug-related offense and have either failed a drug test or have a recognized substance abuse problem at the time of arrest (King & Pasquarella, 2009). Drug courts emphasize treatment of lower-level drug offenders, although some programs have begun to accept violent offenders—these programs usually require additional monitoring from the courts. Offenders typically are identified in lower-court proceedings and then have their cases transferred to a drug court where a treatment program is determined. While examining New York's coordinated system for providing alternatives to incarceration, researchers from the Vera Institute found that offenders are typically charged with a drug-related offense or robbery, and most are poor, have not graduated high school, are unemployed, have multiple social and health problems, and have prior criminal records (Porter, Lee, & Lutz, 2002).

There are generally two models for drug courts: **deferred prosecution programs** and **post-adjudication programs**. The majority of drug courts use the deferred prosecution model; this model diverts offenders into the drug court system prior to entering a plea to a criminal charge. Those who successfully complete the treatment program are not further prosecuted upon completion. Offenders in post-adjudication programs are required to plead guilty to their charges, but their sentences are deferred or suspended as they participate in the treatment program. After completing the program, offenders must return to criminal court for sentencing for the guilty plea he or she provided; although offenders who successfully complete the post-adjudication program may have their participation in the drug court program expunged from their record.

Drug court programs typically run between six months and one year, though many participants remain in programs for longer. Treatment programs generally include up to three levels or stages (Fulkerson, 2009). Participants begin with detoxification as sobriety is necessary for any subsequent treatment. Participants then progress through various stages of individual and group counseling sessions. Finally, participants continue with aftercare treatment that may include such elements as continued substance use counseling or vocational and life-skills training.

Drug court participants are required to periodically attend status hearings with the judge to ensure they are progressing through their treatment programs. This process is similar to probation, although offenders are not actually sentenced to probation and are seen by the judge rather than a probation officer (Lab et al., 2011). Participants must complete all aspects of their particular program, and successful completion is contingent upon remaining drug free and without arrests for a specified period of time. A participant who is noncompliant with any of the program components can be sanctioned through a variety of means, including increased status hearings, drug tests, or jail time. Some situations, such as an individual refusing to continue participation in a treatment program, could result in removal from the program and possibly lead to an individual being taken into custody.

Judges are able to use their discretion for participants who relapse, as this will be expected from persons who have a history of substance abuse. Participants who relapse into substance use behaviors may be required to repeat one or more levels of the program. However, to be effective, drug courts must perceive relapses as inevitable and prepare a range of judicial responses for dealing with these types of violations.

Positive and Negative
Aspects of Drug Courts

A very positive aspect of drug courts is that they serve a vulnerable population (Tyuse & Linhorst, 2005). For example, one review found that 25% of drug court participants were female, 48% were racial minorities, 74% had previous felony convictions, 49% were unemployed at the time of arrest, 76% had failed earlier drug treatment, 20% had attempted suicide, and between 15% and 56% reported previous physical or sexual abuse. Another positive aspect of drug courts is that they provide alternatives to incarceration through a range of community treatment and support services (Tyuse & Linhorst, 2005). For the criminal justice system, they provide a practical response to the overwhelming number of cases that involve substance abuse problems and the number, as well as the number of inmates. Programs typically offer participants outpatient treatment, access to various support groups, mental health treatment, drug and alcohol prevention, educational and vocational training, and residential services (Peyton & Gossweiler, 2001; Shaffer, et al., 2009).

Drug courts are designed and operated at the local level, which makes direct comparisons difficult. Despite a similar general framework and common set of objectives, individual courts may differ regarding specific selection criteria, protocols for adjudication, means of supervision and revocation procedures, and what works best for their communities. Thus, reports about the effectiveness of drug treatment courts have been mixed. Some evaluations have shown positive results, while others have found little to no impact from participation (King & Pasquarella, 2009; Lab et al., 2011).

Some research has suggested that offenders who graduate from their treatment program have shown to recidivate less than those offenders who were adjudicated in a traditional court. Overall, drug court participants have fewer rearrests, fewer reconvictions, longer periods between arrests, and fewer relapses into substance abuse behaviors (King & Pasquarella, 2009; Lab et al., 2011; Tyuse & Linhorst, 2005). In one study, Shaffer et al. (2009) found that a group of female offenders were significantly less likely to recidivate over a long term follow-up period than those who were processed in traditional court settings. It is important to examine the effectiveness of drug courts for female offenders for several reasons. For instance, men and women use drugs and alcohol for different reasons and experience different consequences from their use. Additionally, treatment programs are often designed to address the needs of male offenders, while the needs of female offenders have largely been ignored. Often, female offenders are subjected to the same services that men receive or are provided treatment that is sexist in nature—such as programs designed to increase the offender's domestic capabilities (Shaffer et al., 2009).

Evaluations of drug courts generally show that drug courts are less expensive than incarceration and simple probation. This primarily occurs because of decreases in the number of arrests, case processing, jail occupancy, and the costs of victimization. While it is not certain that everyone who is diverted to drug court treatment would have been sentenced to incarceration, the difference in costs is still worth mentioning. The average annual cost per inmate is generally estimated at $23,000, while the average annual cost of drug court treatment is estimated at $4,300 per person (King & Pasquarella, 2009).

There are also some concerns related to the use and effectiveness of drug courts. Although drug courts serve a vulnerable population, they can only serve a limited number of individuals with substance abuse problems and have a limited amount of resources available. A number of courts have been created in recent years; yet many jurisdictions are still without drug courts because of a lack of funding and other treatment resources or because of resistance from some judges or prosecutors (Goldkamp & Irons-Guynn, 2000; Peyton & Gossweiler, 2001; Tyuse & Linhorst, 2005).

Another concern relates to targeting offenders for participation in drug courts. Some critics have argued that drug courts select candidates whom they perceive will be successful in treatment as opposed to those they believe will fail, a process referred to as **selective participation** (Peyton & Gossweiler,

Table 2: The Ten Essential Elements of Mental Health Courts

1. *Planning and Administration*–A broad-based group of stakeholders representing the criminal justice, mental health, substance abuse treatment, and related systems and the community guides the planning and administration of the court.

2. *Target Population*–Eligibility criteria address public safety and consider a community's treatment capacity, in addition to the availability of alternatives to pretrial detention for defendants with mental illness. Eligibility criteria also take into account the relationship between mental illness and a defendant's offenses, while allowing the individual circumstances of each case to be considered.

3. *Timely Participant Identification and Linkage to Services*–Participants are identified, referred, and accepted into mental health courts, and then linked to community-based service providers as quickly as possible.

4. *Terms of Participation*–Terms of participation are clear, promote public safety, facilitate the defendant's engagement in treatment, are individualized to correspond to the level of risk that the defendant presents to the community, and provide for positive legal outcomes for those individuals who successfully complete the program.

5. *Informed Choice*–Defendants fully understand the program requirements before agreeing to participate in a mental health court. They are provided legal counsel to inform this decision and subsequent decisions about program involvement. Procedures exist in the mental health court to address, in a timely fashion, concerns about a defendant's competency whenever they arise.

6. *Treatment Supports and Services*–Mental health courts connect participants to comprehensive and individualized treatment supports and services in the community. They strive to use— and increase the availability of—treatment and services that are evidenced based.

7. *Confidentiality*–Health and legal information should be shared in a way that potential participants' confidentiality rights as mental health consumers and their constitutional rights as defendants are assured. Information gathered as part of the participants' court-ordered treatment program or services should be safeguarded in the event that participants are returned to traditional court processing.

8. *Court Team*–A team of criminal justice and mental health staff and service and treatment providers receives special, ongoing training and helps mental health court participants achieve treatment and criminal justice goals by regularly reviewing and revising the court process.

9. *Monitoring Adherence to Court Requirements*–Criminal justice and mental health staff collaboratively monitor participants' adherence to court conditions, offer individualized graduated incentives and sanctions, and modify treatment as necessary to promote public safety and participants' recovery.

10. *Sustainability*–Data are collected and analyzed to demonstrate the impact of the mental health court; its performance is assessed periodically (and procedures are modified accordingly); court processes are institutionalized; and support for the court in the community is cultivated and expanded.

Source: Thompson, Osher, & Tomasini-Joshi (2007). *Improving responses to people with mental illnesses: The essential elements of a mental health court.*

2001). In fact, many drug courts do not select those who appear to lack motivation or those who also suffer from mental illness.

Once an offender has been deemed eligible for drug court treatment, his or her participation is voluntary. Some critics argue that the effectiveness from some evaluations could be attributed to this voluntary component (Lab et al., 2011; Tyuse & Linhorst, 2005). In other words, offenders who choose to participate in the drug court treatment option are possibly more motivated to be successful than those who choose otherwise. Critics further argue there is an inherent element of coercion that exists when forcing offenders to choose between jail and participation in treatment. This coercive element is likely intensified when the adversarial process is set aside for courtroom personnel to collectively suggest treatment for an offender. Interestingly, the same argument could be made in traditional court models when considering the number of cases resolved through the process of plea bargaining.

A major criticism of drug courts is their perceived punitive nature (King & Pasquarella, 2009; Stinchcomb, 2010). For example, the Vera Institute of Justice has raised concerns that participants in drug court end up spending more time incarcerated than they would have if they were sentenced from a traditional court system. Because most drug court participants are nonviolent offenders, many would receive relatively short sentences. Additional penalties and time are often accrued as a result of sanctions for noncompliance. In addition to the potential for increased time in jail are the demanding features of drug court treatment (Stinchcomb, 2010). For instance, drug court treatment programs require participants to abstain from substance use while submitting to periodic testing, attending counseling sessions, finding employment, reporting to court for status updates, and possibly more depending on their specific treatment plans. Some offenders may consider the demands of drug court treatment as a waste of time when provided with the alternative option of a relatively short sentence. Critics argue that the punitive nature of drug courts has shifted the traditional focus of punishment into the realm of sanctions for noncompliance rather than exchange it for treatment.

A related concern is the notion that drug courts may be increasing the number of arrests for drug crimes instead of decreasing the number of people who are processed by the criminal justice system, a process often referred to as **net-widening** (Lab et al., 2011). This suggests that law enforcement officers will arrest more substance abuse offenders because they have drug court treatment as an alternative option to incarceration. Drug courts are intended to serve as a diversion for those who were likely to be arrested anyway and not as an intermediate sanction between non-adjudication and incarceration.

There are additional concerns that drug courts might allow for existing racial disparities in the criminal justice system to continue (King & Pasquarella, 2009). A disadvantage exists for African Americans because eligibility requirements disqualify offenders with a long criminal history or those whose offenses would otherwise result in being sentenced to prison. In addition, a high failure rate exists for most treatment programs, and African Americans tend to fail at a higher rate than whites because of socioeconomic disadvantage. Furthermore, because drug court treatments typically result in more jail or prison time for offenders than traditional court systems, there is a concern that racial disparities in correctional populations will continue.

Another major concern for drug courts is the variation found in outcome evaluations (Tyuse & Linhorst, 2005). Some of this variation occurs because of a lack of methodological rigor. Consider that many variables believed to impact treatment outcomes—such as age, race, gender, socioeconomic status, criminal history, and substance abuse history—are often not included in analyses of drug court treatment programs. There is also considerable variation in completion rates of drug court programs and the number of positive drug screenings that occur. It is important to also note that only about 20% of inmates confined in institutional settings actually participate in alcohol or drug treatment programs (Lab et al., 2011). Inmates that do participate tend to do so during the last six months of their incarceration. Programs that do seem to work are intensive, last nine months to one year, focus on offenders who are younger and more at risk, and continue services after participants are released.

Mental Health Courts

Similar to drug courts, mental health courts were created as a response to the increasing number of offenders with mental illnesses that were being served by criminal courts and correctional facilities in the 1980s and 1990s (Mental Health Courts, 2006; Thompson, Osher, & Tomasini-Joshi, 2007).Various sources report that between 5% and 20% of inmates in jail or prisons suffer from some type of mental illness (Mental Health Courts, 2006; Lab et al., 2011). Inmates with mental illnesses are often difficult to control because correctional officers typically do not have the necessary training or education to deal with these inmates. In addition, inmates with mental illness are generally at more risk for physical and psychological victimization (Lab et al., 2011). More importantly, many inmates do not receive adequate treatment while incarcerated, and many fail to establish aftercare programs once they are released, so they remain untreated and end up cycling again and again through courtrooms, correctional facilities, and local neighborhoods. As a result, court officials, state policy makers, and mental health professionals designed mental health courts (Mental Health Courts, 2006; Lab et al., 2011; Thompson, Osher, & Tomasini-Joshi, 2007).

Mental health courts are modeled after drug courts and also emphasize treatment rather than incarceration (Mental Health Courts, 2006; Lab et al., 2011; Tyuse & Linhorst, 2005). Mental health courts are described as problem-solving courts with a foundation of therapeutic jurisprudence. Differing from traditional courts, judges, prosecutors, defense attorneys, and mental health professionals work together to partner eligible defendants with appropriate treatment providers and community-based supervision (Mental Health Courts, 2006; Thompson, Osher, & Tomasini-Joshi, 2007).

Referrals to mental health court are received from prosecutors, defense attorneys, therapists, and relatives, and defendants can be referred either pre-sentence or post-sentence (Mental Health Courts, 2006; Tyuse & Linhorst, 2005). Eligible defendants can receive a variety of services that may include mental health treatment, substance abuse treatment, medication, psycho-therapy, life skills training, vocational training, housing, treatment for head injuries, treatment for trauma-related injuries, and treatment for aggressive behavior (Mental Health Courts, 2006; Lab et al., 2011; Tyuse & Linhorst, 2005). Defendants may be incarcerated longer than a person would who does not have a mental illness, but it cannot be longer than the maximum sentence for the crime committed, and not more than one to two years total. Judges can return offenders to the criminal justice system for treatment noncompli-ance, but this rarely happens, as public praise or criticism is considered more effective than sanctions. Some courts authorize removal of charges if the defendant successfully completes the program.

Historical Overview of Mental Health Courts

In the 19th century, persons with mental illness were housed in asylums, along with the poor, the criminal, and anyone else deemed unfit for society (Lab et al., 2011). Patients in asylums generally were sedated with tranquilizers so that they were easily controlled. This practice continued into the 20th cen-tury, as long-term institutionalization became the preferred method of care for persons with mental illness. Over time, states created and implemented community mental health acts that led to the deinstitutionalization of these patients (Lab et al., 2011; Tyuse & Linhorst, 2005). Patients who were no longer considered a threat to themselves or to others were released into the community. Although not considered a threat, many of these patients were still unable to function in ways that society finds acceptable; therefore, many were arrested and incarcerated. It is generally accepted that the high number of mental health inmates currently in correctional facilities is a result of the deinstitutionalization process that began in the 1960s.

The idea of mental health courts arose from the popularity of the drug courts. The first mental health court was established in Broward County, Florida, in 1997 (Harvard Mental Health Letter, 2006; Tyuse & Linhorst, 2005). Mental health courts were originally designed for misdemeanors and typically pro-cessed cases for trespassing, drug possession, vandalism, wandering in traffic, and urinating in public; however, some courts have been accepting defendants with violent crime charges, such as burglary, robbery, and aggravated assault. These programs require more supervision and may use jail time as a sanction for noncompliance (Harvard Mental Health Letter, 2006).

Ten Essential Elements
for Mental Health Courts

The number of mental health courts has increased significantly in recent years (Thompson, Osher, and Tomasini-Joshi, 2007). The vast majority of mental health courts include a specialized court docket, which employs a problem-solving approach to court processing; judicially supervised, community-based treatment plans that are developed by a team of court staff and mental health professionals for each defendant participating in the court; regular status hearings that utilize incentives and sanctions to encourage compliance with treatment programs; and criteria defining a participant's completion, or graduation, of the program. Individual courts and treatment programs will differ in some areas, but will function very similar to one another.

Experts do agree, however, that several elements are essential to mental health courts, so that they are able to incorporate the criminal justice system and mental health systems effectively and to ensure that both defendants and the community benefit from their operation. Thompson, Osher, and Tomasini-Joshi (2007) recommend ten essential elements for local communities who are interested in either developing a mental health court or reviewing the organization and functioning of an existing court.

First, mental health courts require planning and administration from a broad group of stakeholders who will also be responsible for various treatment functions. The second element suggests that mental health courts should function to offer options to criminal justice professionals for responding to offenders with mental illness besides arrest and detention. The third element refers to early or quick identification of eligible participants and prompt introduction to treatment services. This element is concerned with applying treatment as quickly as possible. Element four emphasizes terms of participation and recommends that treatment programs be tailored to individual participants. This element is also concerned with making sure that treatment goals are clearly described to participants, especially the consequences that could result from noncompliance. The fifth element is informed choice. Participation in mental health courts is voluntary; however, court personnel are responsible for making sure that eligible participants understand what is expected of them in order to successfully complete the treatment program (Thompson et al., 2007).

Element six, Treatment Supports and Services, refers to mental health courts using a variety of treatment services and programs. A variety of services is used so that treatment can be individualized for participants. The seventh element is Confidentiality and emphasizes defendants' right to privacy. Federal and state laws protect participants' confidentiality of medical, mental health, and substance abuse treatment records. This is particularly important as it protects participants against any stigma, especially if he or she must return to traditional court processing. The eighth element refers to the collective effort that is required from criminal justice professionals, mental health professionals, and treatment providers. Generally speaking, a court team might include a judicial officer, prosecutor, defense counsel, probation officer, and a treatment provider or case manager. The court team will closely monitor the defendant, which is element nine, and report about his or her progress during status hearings. Frequent status hearings allow the court to adjust or modify treatment processes through the use of incentives and sanctions. The final element is sustainability. This element recommends that mental health courts conduct frequent and systematic evaluations so as to make necessary adjustments to ensure effectiveness. It is important to note that each of these elements relies on collaboration from criminal justice professionals, mental health professionals, various treatment providers and professionals, and other related systems (Thompson et al., 2007).

Positive and Negative Aspects of Mental Health Courts

Comparisons of mental health courts are somewhat difficult, as results have provided little evidence about their effectiveness (Mental Health Courts, 2006; Lab et al., 2011). Some studies have reported that offenders have spent fewer days in mental hospitals or jail the following year after participation in treatment programs, and participants in another study reported greater satisfaction with life, improved mental health, and less need for residential drug treatment the following year. Advocates of mental health courts identify several benefits from their use. For instance, mental health courts serve a vulnerable population (Tyuse & Linhorst, 2005). A review of two of the largest mental health courts revealed that approximately 25% of participants were female and about 25% were from racial minority groups, between 25% and 45% had a major mental illness and substance use disorder, over 50% were not receiving mental health treatment at the time of their arrest, most were receiving disability income, and about 25% were homeless at the time of their arrest (Goldkamp & Irons-Guynn, 2000).

Mental health courts also provide alternatives to incarceration (Tyuse & Linhorst, 2005). This is particularly important, as incarceration often intensifies psychiatric symptoms for inmates with mental illness. In addition, inmates with mental illness are often at greater risk for physical and sexual victimization and suicide. Advocates additionally argue that mental health courts are beneficial because they provide a range of services that can be adapted to individual defendants and communities, and also serve as an improvement to simple diversion from the criminal justice system because a defendant's progress is closely monitored by the courts (Mental Health Courts, 2006; Tyuse & Linhorst, 2005, Shaffer et al., 2009). Finally, advocates argue that even though treatment can only last for one or two years at most, offenders may decide to continue treatment on their own after experiencing some of the benefits.

Critics of mental health courts argue that they serve a limited number of people and some jurisdictions suffer from limited resources (Tyuse & Linhorst, 2005). Critics also argue that mental health courts have no real power to make sure that participants are receiving adequate and appropriate treatment, and in some cases the necessary resources for treatment may not be available (Mental Health Courts, 2006). These problems will persist as long as the social, political, and economic climates continue to favor more punitive responses to crime.

Critics also fear that mental health courts will persuade law enforcement officers to arrest mentally ill persons as a way to get them the treatment they need, which could unnecessarily stigmatize them. This may explain why some critics favor the use of mental health courts for those who commit felonies rather than misdemeanors (Mental Health Courts, 2006). They argue that mental health court alternatives for felony law violators is more legally and morally acceptable because these offenders are otherwise not eligible for diversionary programs. Critics further argue that mentally ill defendants are not able to genuinely volunteer, or make a competent and informed choice. This is important for situations where a defendant is required to enter a guilty plea because of his or her mental illness, whereas an offender who is not mentally ill could have the charges dismissed. Finally, critics argue that participation in mental health courts can stigmatize defendants, even more so if they return to traditional court processing.

Conclusion

Without a doubt, courtrooms and correctional facilities have faced an increase in the number of offenders that require special assistance and programming. However, many jails and prisons do not provide adequate treatment for substance abuse or mental illness while offenders are incarcerated, and few provide aftercare once they are released (Lab et al., 2011). As an example, Karl & Pasquarella (2009) reported that in 2004, 53% of state prison inmates were identified as having a drug abuse problem, but only 15% were receiving professional treatment. In addition, inmates with mental illness are considered to be at higher risk for physical and psychological victimization. Further compounding the problem for jails and prisons is that many correctional officers do not have the necessary training or educational background to deal with inmates that have substance abuse problems or mental health problems. Some jurisdictions have specialized prisons that primarily house inmates with specific characteristics that pose unique challenges to institutions (Lab et al., 2011).

Despite the progress that our traditional institutions have made regarding screening, services, and treatment, there is a need for more improvements. Drug courts and mental health courts represent a fundamental change in the way courts do business and in the way courts address offenders with substance abuse problems and mental illness. This fundamental change requires a significant effort on the part of criminal justice and treatment professionals to step outside traditional practices and procedures to achieve a non-adversarial, problem-solving approach for treating offenders with substance abuse problems or mental illness.

References

About the drug courts program office. (2000, June). *Drug Courts Program Office*. U.S. Department of Justice.

Clark, C. L., Aziz, D. W., & MacKenzie, D. L. (1994). *Shock incarceration in New York: Focus on treatment*. National Institute of Justice. Retrieved from https://www.ncjrs.gov/pdffiles/shockny.pdf

Cosden, M., Baker, A., Benki, C., Patz, S., Walker, S., & Sullivan, K. (2010). Consumers' perspectives on successful and unsuccessful experiences in a drug treatment court. *Substance Use & Misuse, 45* 1033–1049.

DeMatteo, D. (2010). A proposed prevention intervention for non–drug-dependent drug court clients. *Journal of Cognitive Psychotherapy: An International Quarterly, 24* (2) 104–115. doi: 10.1891/0889-8391.24.2.104

Fulkerson, A. (2009). The drug treatment court as a form of restorative justice. *Contemporary Justice Review, 12* (3), 253–267. doi: 10.1080/10282580903105772

Goldkamp, J. S. & Irons-Guynn, C. (2000). *Emerging judicial strategies for the mentally ill in the criminal caseload: Mental health courts in Fort Lauderdale, Seattle, San Bernardino, and Anchorage*. U.S. Department of Justice. Retrieved from http://www.ncjrs.gov/App/Publications

Hora, P. F. (2002). A dozen years of drug treatment courts: Uncovering our theoretical foundation and the construction of a mainstream paradigm. *Substance Use & Misuse, 37* (12 & 13), 1469–1488. doi: 10.108/JA-1200449

King, R. S. & Pasquarella, J. (2009). *Drug courts: A review of the evidence*. The Sentencing Project. Retrieved from http://www.sentencingproject.org

Lab, S. P., Williams, M. R., Holcomb, J. E., Burek, M. W., & Buerger, M. E. (2011). *Criminal Justice: The Essentials* (2nd ed.). New York: Oxford University Press.

Mental Health Courts. (2006, August). *Harvard Mental Health Letter*. Retrieved from http://www.health.harvard.edu

National Criminal Justice Reference Service (NCJRS). (2011). Retrieved from https://www.ncjrs.gov/spotlight/drug_courts/summary.html

Peyton, E. A., & Gossweiler, R. (2001). *Executive summary: Treatment services in adult drug courts*. U.S. Department of Justice. Retrieved from http://www.ncjrs.gov/pdf-files1/bja/188086.pdf

Porter, R., Lee, S., & Lutz, M. (2002). Balancing punishment and treatment: Alternatives to incarceration in New York City. Vera Institute of Justice. Retrieved from http://www.vera.org

Shaffer, D. K., Hartman, J. L., & Listwan, S. J. (2009). Drug-abusing women in the community: The impact of drug court involvement on recidivism. *Journal of Drug Issues*. 803–827.

Stafford, K. P., & Wygant, D. B. (2005). The role of competency to stand trial in mental health courts. *Behavioral Sciences and the Law, 23*, 245–258. doi: 10.1002/bsl.649

Stinchcomb, J. B. (2010). Drug courts: Conceptual foundation, empirical findings, and policy implications. *Drugs: Education, Prevention and Policy, 17* (2), 148–67.

Thompson, M., Osher, F., & Tomasini-Joshi, D. (2007). *Improving responses to people with mental illnesses: The essential elements of a mental health court*. Bureau of Justice Assistance.

Tyuse, S. W., & Linhorst, D. M. (2005). Drug courts and mental health courts: Implications for social work. *Health & Social Work*, 30(3), 233–240.

Vrecko, S. (2009). Therapeutic justice in drug courts: Crime, punishment and societies of control. *Science as Culture, 18* (2), 217–232.

Learn More on the Internet:

National Association of Drug Court Professionals:
http://www.nadcp.org/learn/what-are-drug-courts
Drug Court Video from Roanoke, Virginia:
http://www.youtube.com/watch?v=x_YE8Tt0e4A
Frontline: Inside a Mental Health Court:
http://www.pbs.org/wgbh/pages/frontline/released/inside/

Discussion Questions:

1. Is there a need for drug courts and mental health courts within the criminal justice system, or should these offenders be processed with everyone else?

2. Should the idea of specialty courts be expanded to other types of offenders or crimes? If no, explain why not. If yes, explain what types of offenders or crimes might be appropriate.

Chapter Six

Prosecutorial Discretion

By Isis N. Walton and Shanieka S. Jones

Introduction

T he organization of the criminal justice system consists of a sequence of decision points in three major crime control agencies—police, courts, and corrections. Each agency makes a decision to keep or release individuals from the system. Although these crime control agencies make up the structure of the system, they do not make decisions; it is only the framework for decision making. The process through which criminal justice is handled involves a lot of decision making by criminal justice professionals within these agencies. The major goals of this chapter are to understand the impact of prosecutorial power, specifically focusing on the level of discretion prosecutors possess and examine how various processes, procedures, and policies impact prosecutorial discretion. Of particular note, this chapter will focus on the impact prosecutorial discretion has on plea bargaining as it relates to race and gender, mandatory minimums, and peremptory challenges.

The Decision-Making Process

Discretion, also known as legal judgment, is a major part of the criminal justice system (Neubauer, 2005). It is defined as the ability of a governmental agent to exercise lawful decision making that fits within his or her occupational capacity in hopes of making a determination (Neubauer, 2005). Police discretion differs from a judge's discretion, and they both differ from prosecutorial discretion. Each agent's discretion is determined by his or her role in the criminal justice system. In addition to legal judgment, there are two other subcomponents of discretion: **policy priorities** and **personal philosophies** (Cole, 1970; Neubauer, 2005). A police officer determines whether to give a warning, write a summons, or make an arrest based on the situation. In terms of policy priority, the number of crimes a single person could be charged with is virtually unlimited, but resources are not (Neubauer, 2005). Therefore, discretion is used to determine which crimes take precedence over others. Moreover, discretion can be influenced by someone's personal philosophy (Neubauer, 2005). Judges and prosecutors have different outlooks on what constitutes a serious offense and what arbitrates high priority (Neubauer, 2005). A case may be postponed or bail may not be set as high as the prosecutor requests if a judge does not agree to the severity of threat the accused is claimed to pose to the community or to the case if released during trial.

The Formal Process of Crime Control Agencies: "Producers and Products"

Within the criminal justice system, the court is considered the "hub," where all law enforcement and prosecutorial agents work to move defendants through the court system. This movement (process) of a defendant through the system concludes with a "product"-making process. This process changes the legal statuses of people, thereby creating "products" ranging from suspects, to defendants, offenders, and finally to ex offenders (Remington et al., 1982). However, it is this process of movement—a complex web of "ebbs and flows" and the interdependent decision making by all agencies, especially the prosecutor—which warrants special attention. Although it can be diagrammed very basically (as seen in Diagram 1), the process of criminal prosecution is one that requires multilevel compliance and cooperation.

In its basic analysis, the process is as follows. Law enforcement agencies are responsible for arresting individuals (suspects) who allegedly commit crimes. Prosecutors are responsible for determining whether or not to prosecute (via prosecutorial discretion). If the decision is made to prosecute, suspects are defendants. Courts determine whether one is guilty or not guilty to ensure the defendant's constitutional rights and administer punishment if found guilty (offender). Corrections carry out the punishment of the offender and produce ex offenders when released from supervision (Remington et al., 1982). Within this system, the judge has considerable power. However, it is the power that the prosecutor possesses that will serve as the central focus of this chapter.

Figure 1: Court as "hub" of criminal justice system

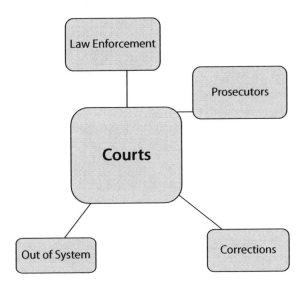

Who Determines the Charges?

A common misperception with students is the belief that police have the greatest degree of power in criminal processing. First- and second-year criminal justice students as well as non-majors often think that police determine the charges that will be brought against the offender. When in reality, it is actually the prosecutor in conjunction with the police who determines the charges. Sometimes this process is not quite evident or easy to understand.

Between law enforcement and the court lies the prosecutorial department (i.e., district attorneys, county and city attorneys, and U.S. Attorneys) whose duty includes drawing up charging documents presented to the courts. Public defenders and defense counsel are also included.

After the initial arrest, the prosecutor is responsible for deciding to proceed with the case or drop it after reviewing police reports, and in some cases, talking with officers. Arrest and booking does not guarantee criminal processing of a suspect. The prosecutor may decide not to prosecute and/or reduce the charges, because there is not sufficient evidence to prove the charges beyond a reasonable doubt. This power is called prosecutorial discretion.

Is the prosecutor a law enforcement agent or a court work group agent? He/she is a lawyer, a court work group agent who works closely with law enforcement to bring the case to trial and secure a conviction.

Prosecutorial Discretion

The modern prosecuting attorney in the United States exercises unregulated discretion in three areas crucial to trying a case (Albonetti, 1987). They determine the circumstances under which charges are filed, the charges the accused will incur, and if the case is suitable for trial. If it is not suitable, they decide to discontinue prosecuting (Albonetti, 1987; Carp et al., 2007). Prosecutorial discretion usually begins once a police report is forwarded to the county or state attorney for review. The prosecutor reviews and assesses the details of the case and the evidence in order to conclude whether the situation is severe enough and if the evidence is direct enough to bring forth charges (Neubauer, 2005; Carp et al., 2007). If it is decided that charges are to be brought, the process of selective prosecution begins. **Selective prosecution** entails the "absolute and unrestricted" right of the prosecution to decide who is and is not prosecuted (Inciardi, 2000). Caulfield (1989) indicated factors that influence this decision to "include the nature of the offense, the characteristics of the offender, the age of the offender, the interests of the offender, and possible improper motives of a victim or witness" (p. 234). However, all selective processes must have justification.

The decision to go forth to trial depends on the size of the court's caseload, the severity of the case, and ambiguity in the law (Carp et al., 2007). Reversely, the decision not to press charges may be supported by the fact that court and investigative resources should be better used toward a more serious case. Furthermore, attaching criminal charges to a person who is considered a subsidiary offender may cause more harm than good by starting them on the path to becoming a habitual offender (Caulfield, 1989). Large numbers of arrests are for criminal offenses that are offensive and publicly disturbing rather than truly devastating to the welfare of the community, such as drunkenness and disorderly conduct (Inciardi, 2000). Prosecuting these cases is considered a waste of time and viewed as not beneficial to the community. The decision to prosecute is usually based on the two aforementioned extremes, minor offenses and major offenses that endanger the welfare of the community. However, if there is a case that falls in between the two, then the prosecution must predetermine if going forward is worth it, does the benefit of prosecuting outweigh the costs (Carp et al., 2007).

There are multiple groups who place pressure on the prosecution as they make the decision whether or not to prosecute. Law enforcement, courts, the community (including media's perception), and defense attorneys constantly infringe upon the prosecutor's discretion (Cole, 1970; Poole & Regoli, 1983; Caulfield, 1989; Carp et al., 2007). Police officers may pressure prosecution not to pursue a case because the suspect has information that may lead to the prosecution and closing of a bigger case and is willing to cooperate. Judges may be disinclined to convict because of prison overcrowding, which ultimately affects whether the prosecutor will go forth since they know that there is a great chance they will not get the sentence they are requesting. Since county, state, and district attorneys are appointed or elected, they favor specific types of offenders and offenses to please the community and adhere to their communal concerns (Carp et al., 2007). If the accused has a criminal record, the chance the prosecutor will file charges increases.

Perhaps the most powerful type of discretionary power a prosecutor possesses is that of *nolle prosequi*, which, according to Inciardi (2000), is the "formal entry in the record by which the prosecutor declares that he or she will no longer prosecute the case, either (1) as to some of the counts, (2) as to some of the defendants, or (3) altogether" (p. 344). A prosecutor may decide to enter nolle prosequi if evidence is later deemed insufficient or has been determined inadmissible once trial has begun (Joseph, 1975; Inciardi, 2000). Nolle prosequi prevents trivial cases from going to court, eliminates false accusations, and removes cases in which the prosecution is guaranteed to lose; however, it can lead to discrimination and corruption (Carp et al., 2007).

Plea bargaining, although frowned upon by victims and law enforcement, is a necessary method because all cases cannot go to trial due to budgetary constraints and lack of resources. Objections arise because the offender is not punished to fullest extent of the law when pleas are accepted. Why do prosecutors offer defendants the opportunity to plead guilty to lesser charges?

Negotiated Justice: Plea Bargaining

One of the most commonly used practices regarding prosecutorial discretion is plea negotiations, better known as plea bargaining (Carp et al., 2007). **Plea bargaining** is a pretrial activity that is used for a variety of reasons, including ensuring the defendant, who has committed a crime, is brought to justice. These reasons can range from resource constraints, to lack of enough evidence, and non-credible witnesses. Whatever the reason, the prosecutor has a significant amount of power to make this decision with or without the consultation of others.

Negotiations, however, are usually made between the prosecutor and the defense attorney and/or the defendant in hopes to arrive at an agreement, where the defendant will receive judicial concession if he or she pleads guilty to his or her accused crime and/or cooperate in the prosecution's investigation of another case (Carp et al., 2007). Types of concessions include: (1) the initial charges may be reduced or dropped; (2) the number of counts may be reduced in instances where there are multiple charges; (3) a recommendation for leniency may be made by the prosecutor; and (4) a complaint may be changed to a less disturbing one in cases where labels are attached, such as a child molestation being called assault (Rosett & Cressey,1976; McCoy, 1993). The key is not to conclude the defendant as guilty or innocent, but the case's strength (Reinganum, 1988). A prosecutor could have a weak case against someone who is guilty but an extremely strong case against someone who is innocent.

The Impact of Race and Gender in Plea Bargaining

The level of discretion that prosecutors have in offering pleas is problematic. Race and gender may play a significant role in how prosecutors see a defendant's level of criminality, or more specifically the degree to which they are innocent or guilty. As we consider this analogy, it is important to understand that "multiple marginality" (Chesney-Lind, 1997, p. 4) is an ongoing process that involves continuous oppressive forces of racism, classism, and sexism (van Wormer and Bartollas, 2007). Multiple marginality is not just the layering effect of these oppressive forces, but requires a more conscious careful analysis that takes into consideration each oppressive force has a collateral impact and effect on one another (van Wormer and Bartollas, 2007).

Race can produce a false positive effect in plea bargaining where the prosecutor's biases keeps him/her from offering a plea deal to a person of color, due to his/her social construction of knowledge. The prosecutor, through the use of media images and other ideological forming mediums, may be "used to" seeing Blacks and Hispanics as criminal offenders and may not offer a plea. Unintentional and unconscious as it may be, the formation of such knowledge conveys the acceptance of the "normalcy of criminalization" (Unnever & Gabbidon, 2011) for certain individuals—namely minorities—without the consideration of the collateral impact of sending record numbers of people from disadvantaged communities to prison (Walton, 2011). In these situations, the prosecutor may internalize sending these offenders to jail or prison as a way of "saving a life" and better than the alternative of leaving them in disadvantaged and crime-ridden communities.

On the other hand, race can also produce a positive negative effect, in that a prosecutor's decision to offer a plea *based on his/her belief that it is more beneficial due to defendant's relative situation*. In other words, prosecutors may offer plea bargains to lower-class African American defendants as leverage because of their inability to pay for legal counsel. For many, the idea of taking the plea in exchange for lesser charges may be a more viable option than going to trial with a public defender who "works" for the system, despite their actual innocence or guilt. In regard to gender, women may be offered more chances for plea bargaining even when the crime they have committed may be more severe. This may have to do with the notion that women have been regarded as a group that needs protection and preferential treatment (Pollock, 2002; van Wormer & Bartollas, 2007). Further, for many, because women are "mothers" or maternal, this role minimizes their threat level.

Women collectively as a group have been afforded protection from the male criminal justice system and excused for their criminal actions (Pollock, 2002; van Wormer & Bartollas, 2007). This notion is known as the **chivalry hypothesis**. Although research (Daly, 1994) has not been conclusive in this area indicating women have significantly benefited from chivalry, other research has concluded that chivalry has had a moderate effect, especially when taking a historical analysis into context (Pollock, 2002). White women have often benefited from this preferential treatment, while Black and Hispanic women are not always offered this same level of consideration, as they are "seen less deserving and/or perceived as less 'feminine'" (Pollock, 2002, p. 41). Farnworth & Teske (1995) referred to this idea as "**selective chivalry**," which refers to the extension of disproportionate chivalry or preferential treatment by decision makers to white women during criminal prosecution. Therefore, the intersection of race, class, and stereotypic images of who constitutes a "woman" or the "virtue of womanhood" must be considered when examining female offenders in the criminal justice system.

Research on women and the criminal justice system must also include the role and impact of patriarchy. This domination and control by males has often led to discriminatory practices against women who are "deemed" troublesome or who commit crimes that are viewed as typical male crimes (van Wormer & Bartollas, 2007). In other words, a female may commit a crime that is traditionally seen as male oriented and her being an "unusual suspect" may be the reason she may not be offered a plea, and in fact may be cause for harsher treatment. For example, the "War on Drugs," can be identified as the single most catastrophic culprit of disparate treatment and the reason for record numbers of minorities in the system (Unnever & Gabbidon, 2011). At the end of 2010, 133 African American women per 100,000 of the U.S.

Black population were behind bars, in comparison to 47 white women per 100,000 of the white U.S. population and 77 Hispanic women per 100,000 of the Latino U.S. population (Lowe, 2012). Specifically, the increased "federalization" of drug crimes, have particularly impacted Black and brown women disproportionately, as the total number of women sent to prison for drug crimes increased tenfold from 1986 to 1996 (Mauer, Potler, and Wolf, 2000). Current estimates indicated that the incarceration rate for drug offenses of Black women was much higher, when compared with both white and Hispanic women (Lowe, 2012). The real question to be asked is, Do African American women participate in crime more than Caucasian or Latino women? Or are Black women viewed differently than other women, and as a result are treated differently? The answer, according to who answers, varies. Studies indicate that Black women perceive that they are treated differently by the system because of their race in comparison to other women and that in part this treatment is because some—namely prosecutors and other agents of the criminal justice system—"think less of them because they live in or near a stereotypical racialized-criminalized 'ghetto'" (Unnever & Gabbidon, 2011, p. 110).

What is clear is that women who are charged with drug-related crimes are hit just as hard, if not harder, by the increased use of mandatory minimums, determined sentencing structures, and "federalization" of drug crimes (Raeder, 1993a&b; Pollock, 2002). These women, mostly African and Latino Americans, are not the major players or "queenpins." Realistically, most of them have minor involvement in drug rings and thus have less negotiating and/or bargaining power with prosecutors because they have little information to trade. Consequently, they are at the whim of prosecutors and public defendants, as most of them are from lower socioeconomic classes. They end up facing excessive time in prison; meanwhile, their male counterparts receive reduced sentences in return for their testimony (Pollock, 2002; van Wormer & Bartollas, 2007).

Two other points that must be considered concerning race and gender in plea bargaining are: 1) indigent offenders; and 2) the use of plea bargaining to reduce court workload. Indigent offenders may not be able to afford bail and/or afford an attorney and see the plea as their most viable option to be released from jail and not be subjected to other forms of more severe punishment. Prosecutors also consider plea bargaining to help aid in expediency and the backlogging of cases, which help funnel some of the trivial cases out of the system. In both of the above-mentioned cases, there are equally positive and negative outcomes.

Due to the hidden nature of prosecutorial adjudication, prosecutors are not held to the same standards as common due process (Vorenberg, 1981). They can impose the harshest punishment based on personal judgment. Differential treatment, such as prison versus probation, does not have to be rational or consistent and there is no basis or precedent, if you will, to serve as a guide for all cases and defendants with similarities to increase the likelihood of fairness (Vorenberg, 1981). Discretion that lacks the necessary standards to regulate its equality gives prosecutors the power to impose or withhold punishment, subsequently underlining the notion that "society's most fundamental sanctions will be imposed arbitrarily and capriciously and that the least favored members of the community—racial and ethnic minorities, social outcasts, the poor—will be treated most harshly" (Vorenberg, 1981, p. 1555). In terms of plea bargaining, it is more expensive to prosecute homicide and white-collar crimes that involve lengthy investigations and trials than crimes of a smaller scale, for example, narcotics distribution on an individual level. Therefore, low-level crimes and poor defendants see less prosecution (Savitsky, 2009). However, the quality of one's counsel depends on income (Nellis, 2011), so plea bargaining is more often unfavorable for African American defendants than their white counterparts (Savitsky, 2009), since African American defendants tend to be poorer and more likely to experience unwilling and/or inadequate counsel (Nellis, 2011). Innocent white defendants have faith in the criminal justice system and believe that it will work to their benefit. Therefore, they are unlikely to plea bargain since there is no incentive to do so. Even if guilty, a white defendant has enough confidence they will receive a fair trial relying on the perception that it takes more than just guilt to convict. However, even if a white defendant takes a plea, they are more likely to receive more concessions than an African American defendant (Savitsky, 2009). Conversely, whether innocent or guilty, an African American defendant is likely to take a plea bargain because they lack similar faith in the criminal justice system and are more likely to believe the system is out to prove them guilty regardless of involvement and the severity of the crime. Therefore, African Americans are more likely to try to negotiate a deal they see as less uncompromising as compared to what would be given had they gone to trial.

Backlogs of caseloads are not an uncommon problem in the courts. Counsel and judges apply mass-production techniques to combat and minimize the insurmountable amount of cases courts face, for example, **group processing** and **actor specialization** (Neubauer, 2005). Group processing refers to felony defendants being read their rights in a group rather than individually at their initial appearance, while actor specialization is when representatives from the public defender's office take on one specific task, whether it be the initial interview, representing their client at their initial hearing, or negotiating the plea in order to spread the workload (Neubauer, 2005). As mentioned earlier, prosecutors resolve cases with guilty pleas to reduce caseloads, building their conviction rate. This is a significant achievement especially, where cases are weak and the defendant may have been found innocent if the case had gone to trial. Prosecutors also can stack numerous charges to use later as a negotiating tactic. In return for a guilty plea, a prosecutor will drop all but one charge, all the while using their power to manipulate the defendant. Using plea bargaining simply disposes of lesser cases, reduces case backlogs, and allows judges to focuses on more serious matters. However, the "caseload hypothesis" does not explain why the use of plea bargaining is just as ubiquitous in a court with few cases as it is in a court with many cases (Neubauer, 2005).

Plea Bargaining, Mandatory Minimums, and Sentencing

In many states, it is solely the prosecutor's decision to impose **mandatory minimum statutes** (Ulmer, Kurlychek, & Kramer, 2007). The establishment of mandatory minimums was created for equity and fairness in sentencing and punishment for selected offenses (i.e. guns, drugs) and its intended consequence was to remove judicial discretion (FAMM, n. d). Ulmer, Kurlychek, & Kramer (2007) argue that "mandatory-minimum sentencing policies and the consequent displacement of discretion from judges to prosecutors reflect a larger political trend toward distrust of and disempowerment of judges and, simultaneously, growth in the trust in and empowerment of prosecutors" (pp. 427–28).

The 2007 study by Ulmer, Kurlychek, & Kramer adds to the dearth of literature on mandatory minimums (MMs) by analyzing the effect of MMs on prosecutorial sentencing. This study confirmed that mandatory minimums target offenses disproportionately committed by minorities (Tonry, 1992; Rose and Clear, 1998; Beckett and Sasson, 2000), and the prosecutor's discretion to apply mandatory minimums are also biased against minorities.

Bjerk (2005) and Farrell (2003) also provided evidence in their research that extralegal factors play a role in how prosecutors use their discretion to apply mandatory minimums disproportionately to minorities. Bjerk (2005) found that the circumvention of three-strikes mandatories was not proportional or equal for all defendants due to charge reduction discretion by prosecutors. Further, he contended that the circumvented process was judiciously less likely to occur for Hispanic defendants. Other research, such as Kautt and DeLone (2006) concluded that gender played a significant role in sentence severity among federal drug cases where females received less severe sentences than mandatory minimums and those sentenced under the guidelines. Conclusively, the above-mentioned research studies identify a high potential of the disparate application of mandatory minimums by prosecutors.

Bjerk (2005) indicated that plea bargaining has dramatic effects on sentencing, mandatory minimum sentencing in particular. Convictions for crimes targeted by sentencing laws differ tremendously from convictions for a lesser but related crime. Regarding three-strikes laws, Bjerk (2005) found that prosecutors are almost two times as likely to lessen a felony charge to a misdemeanor when conviction on the initial arrest would fall under three-strikes sentencing. Moreover, these decisions are not a result of criminal, judge, jury, and defense lawyer behavior, but are done simply because of the prosecutor's own predilections and limited resources. Overall, prosecutors are inclined to keep more serious offenders out of the community. Therefore, the use of prosecutorial discretion to evade three-strikes laws is rarer than using prosecutorial discretion to evade mandatory minimums for less serious offenses (Bjerk, 2005).

Peremptory Challenges

Criminal trials are powerful symbols of right versus wrong, good versus evil, and are exceptional examples that publicly teach lessons of honesty, equality, and the efficiency of the criminal justice process. Criminal trials also search for the truth with the burden of proof on the government to prove beyond a reasonable doubt that the defendant is guilty. In this adversarial display of melodrama, the team with the most resources usually reigns victorious. So, when the decision is made to take a defendant to trial, both prosecutors and defense attorneys conjure up their considerable power. Part of this power that prosecutors have is to use ways to eliminate jurors that are unfavorable to them in their quest to bring the defendant to justice.

Juries are important to the process of justice because they are meant to represent the perspectives and opinions of the general society without favoritism (Mahoney, 1982). However, jury pools have yet to reach out in the same way for minorities, young adults, and women as they do for their counterparts. Furthering the exclusion and contributing to the problem of unfair and partial juries is the process of **voir dire**, the actual selection of the specific jury panelists that will serve and ultimately decide the guilt or innocence of the defendant. During voir dire, prospective jurors, or the **venire**, face preliminary examinations in which they are asked questions about their backgrounds, familiarity with any persons involved in the case, and their attitudes about any facts that may be brought to attention during the actual trial (Grossman, 1994; Neubauer, 2005). Based on their responses, they are either kept to serve or eliminated from participating (Buckless and Peace, 1993).

Two conditions used for eliminating jurors are a **challenge for cause** and a **peremptory challenge** (Lieberman, 2011). A prospective juror is eliminated via challenge for cause if that juror's attitude, behavior, and/ or experience demonstrates he or she is biased; therefore, it is extremely unlikely that person will be able to render an impartial verdict (Sommers and Norton, 2007; Lieberman, 2011). Conversely, a peremptory challenge eliminates a prospective juror from consideration without good reason (Sommers and Norton, 2007; Lieberman, 2011). Although the use of peremptory challenges are restricted from allowing a trial lawyer to discriminate, for example, by race, it is hard to believe that this never happens when Blacks continue to be overly ruled out as those who serve on a jury (Lieberman, 2011). Strategies are used to guide voir dire decisions—for example, trial lawyers may rely on their own beliefs about income, occupation, religion, and appearance in determining which persons are best served to their case (Lieberman, 2011). Ultimately though, it is not in a trial lawyer's best interest to obtain an unbiased jury, but rather one that will favor his or her client (Mahoney, 1982).

If there is suspicion that an attorney is inappropriately challenging a prospective juror, they must provide a race-neutral justification to avoid being sanctioned (Sommers and Norton, 2007; Lieberman, 2011). This is known as a **Batson challenge** (Neubauer, 2005; Sommers and Norton, 2007). In the case of *Batson v. Kentucky* (1986), prosecutors were restricted from using peremptory challenges to keep Black Americans from serving on juries where a Black American was the defendant (Neubauer, 2005). A Batson challenge involves three steps: (1) an attorney, prosecution, or defense, challenging one or more of the other's strikes by demonstrating a prima facie case of discrimination; (2) if a prima facie case is established, the counsel that offered the challenged strike must provide a race-neutral justification; and (3) the judge must decide whether the peremptory challenge was motivated by race or gender discrimination, thus sustaining or overruling the challenge (Buckless and Peace, 1993; Sommers and Norton, 2007). Although well intentioned, race-neutral justifications in implementation have amounted to nothing more than creatively arranged terms that "effectively mask the biasing effects of race" (Sommers and Norton, 2007, p. 261). In 1994, Batson was extended to cover gender discrimination in the case of *J. E. B., Petitioner v. Alabama*, where it was declared that using peremptory challenges as a means of gender discrimination in jury selection violated the Equal Protection clause of the Fourteenth Amendment (Grossman, 1994; Neubauer, 2005).

Cultivation Theory: How Real Is the Reach of the Media?

This chapter would be incomplete if it did not at least briefly address the impact of **cultivation theory**, the **mean world syndrome** (MWS), and the impact the media has on the world's view of crime and criminal activity. Despite the declining rates of crime for nearly two decades, more people believe that crime is more pervasive and rampant than ever before. This perception of crime is not surprising given the demand for reality and fictional television shows focused on one or more parts of the criminal justice system.

Cultivation theory proposes that heavy television viewers over time develop worldviews comparable to what they see on television (Gerbner et al., 1980; Morgan & Signorielli, 1990). According to Minnebo & Eggermont (2007) "the cultivation hypothesis was supported when significant differences between light and heavy viewers were found, and when the conceptions of these heavy viewers reflected reality as shown on television" (p. 131). Cultivation theory can impact not only the general public but also the prosecutor and other actors in the criminal justice system. The prosecutor's notion of who is the typical offender is impacted by the media as well as his/her experience with minority defendants. Cultivation theory suggests this could cause the prosecutor to not offer plea bargains to individuals they are "used to" seeing as criminal offenders.

As the demand for reality and fictional court, cop, and criminal justice television shows increases, so too will people's inability to discern the truth about criminal proceedings and crime rates. George Gerbner et al. (1980) coined the term "mean world syndrome" to explain and examine how social knowledge is constructed and applied as television viewing increases and becomes more mainstream. "Mean world syndrome" is the notion that mass media distorts the perception of viewers of violence and violent-related content into believing the world is more dangerous than its actuality, which elicits a need for greater protection than what is necessary by any actual threat (Gerbner et al., 1980). Despite the increased efforts of actors within the criminal justice system and the current reduction in crime rates, people still fear the random stranger as the most dominant criminal assailant. This notion, which is consistently perpetuated on most television shows, refutes reality. Most victims of violent crimes, for example, are assaulted by an acquaintance. The sensationalism of crime shows has contributed to the overall perspective that minority males and increasingly women are dangerous criminal-minded individuals who should be dealt with harshly by the criminal justice system.

Closing Remarks

The criminal justice system is an interconnected structure of processes and flows intertwined with a lot of decision making. In this system, its agencies have distinct roles: for example, police arrest, prosecutors prepare the criminal case for prosecution, court determines guilty or not guilty, and corrections carries out the punishment. However, police and prosecutors must work together to bring charges against the defendant. This is an important step in this process. Prosecutors have an enormous amount of decision-making power known as judicial discretion; put simply it is the power to decide whether or not to charge the defendant and what the charge will be.

The prosecutor's main goal is to seek justice. Often plea bargains are used to this end, where defendants are offered lesser charges for an exchange of a guilty verdict. One negative consequence of pleas is that guilty defendants are not held accountable publicly in court for their actions and only receive partial punishment for their offense. A positive outcome of pleas is that there is an admission of guilt that may not be established if the case were taken to trial. Although there are both negative as well as positive consequences associated with plea bargaining, it is a necessary method used to help expedite cases as well as reduce backlogging of court cases. However, as we continue to empower prosecutors with discretionary power, we must be sure to increase the levels of checks and balances to minimize prosecutorial corruption and discrimination. The use of mandatory minimum sentences and the jury selection process are just two areas of concern where extralegal factors such as race and gender have been reported to be an issue.

Finally, the impact of the media on the prosecutor and jury must be considered. The public is consistently bombarded with media coverage of melodramatic accounts of fictitious criminal shows that present stereotypical images of criminal offenders and levels of criminality. Cultivation theory and mean world syndrome suggest this increased viewing of violent shows will impact the criminal justice system by making it more difficult to acquire impartial and unbiased jurors, maintain fair case management, and distribute equitable justice.

References

Albonetti, C. A. (1987). Prosecutorial Discretion: The Effects of Uncertainty. *Law & Society Review,* 21(2), 291–314.

Albonetti, C. A.. (1991). An Integration of Theories to Explain Judicial Discretion. *Social Problems,* 38, 247–66.

Alozie, N. O. & Johnston, C. W. (2000). Probing the Limits of Female Advantage in Criminal Processing: Pretrial Diversion of Drug Offenders in an Urban County. *Justice System Journal,* 21(3), 239–59.

Beckett, K., & Sasson, T. (2000). *The Politics of Injustice: Crime and Punishment in America.* Thousand Oaks, CA: Pine Forge Press.

Bjerk, D. (2005). Making the Crime Fit the Penalty: The Role of Prosecutorial Discretion under Mandatory Minimum Sentencing. *Journal of Law and Economics,* 48(2), 591–625.

Blumer, H. (1955). Reflections on Theory of Race Relations, pp. 3–21 in *Race Relations in World Perspective*, edited by A. W. Lind. Honolulu: University of Hawaii Press.

Bobo, L. & Hutchings, V. (1996). Perceptions of Racial Group Competition: Extending Blumer's Theory of Group Position to a Multiracial Social Context. *American Sociological Review*, 61, 951–72.

Brereton, D. & Casper, J. (1981). Does It Pay to Plead Guilty? Differential Sentencing and the Functioning of Criminal Courts. *Law and Society Review*, 16(1), 45–70.

Britt, C. (2000). Social Context and Racial Disparities in Punishment Decisions. *Justice Quarterly*, 17(4), 707–32.

Buckless, F. A. & Peace, R. L. (1993). The Influence of the Source of Professional Standards on Juror Decision. *The Accounting Review*, 68(1), 164–75.

Carp, R. A., Stidham, R., & Manning, K. L. (2007). *Judicial Process in America*. Washington, DC: Congressional Quarterly Press.

Caulfield, S. L. (1989). Life or Death Decisions: Prosecutorial Power vs. Equality of Justice. *Journal of Contemporary Criminal Justice*, 5, 233–47.

Cole, G. (1970). The Decision to Prosecute. *Law and Society Review*, vol. 4, pp. 313–43.

Demuth, S. & Steffensmeier, D. (2004). The Impact of Gender and Race-Ethnicity in the Pretrial Release Process. *Social Problems*, 51(2), 222–42.

Chesney-Lind, M. (1997). *The Female Offender: Girls, Women and Crime*. Thousand Oaks, CA: Sage.

Daly, K. (1994). *Gender, Crime and Punishment*. New Haven, CT: Yale University Press.

Engen, R. & Gainey, R. 2000. Modeling the Effects of Legally Relevant and Extra-Legal Factors Under Sentencing Guidelines: The Rules Have Changed. *Criminology*, 38, 1207–30.

Engen, R. & Steen, S. 2000. The Power to Punish: Discretion and Sentencing Reform in the War on Drugs. *American Journal of Sociology*, 105, 1357–95.

Families Against Mandatory Minimums (FAMM). What are mandatory minimums? Available online at http://famm.org/UnderstandSentencing/WhatAreMandatoryMinimums.aspx

Farnworth, M. and Teske, R. H. C. Jr. (1995). Gender differences in felony court processing: Three hypotheses of disparity. *Women and Criminal Justice* 6: 23–44.

Farrell, J. (2003). Mandatory Minimum Firearm Penalties: A Source of Sentencing Disparity. *Justice Research and Policy*, 5(1), 95–115.

Free, M. (2002). Race and Presentencing Decisions in the United States: A Summary and Critique of the Research. *Criminal Justice Review*, 27(2), 203–32.

Gerbner, G., L. Gross, M. Morgan, & N. Signorielli. (1980). The "Mainstreaming" of America: Violence Profile no. 11, *Journal of Communication*, 30(3), 10–29.

Gerbner, G., L. Gross, M. Morgan, & N. Signorielli. (1986). Living with Television: The Dynamics of the Cultivation Process, in Jennings Bryant and Dolf Zillmann (eds.). *Perspectives on Media Effects*, pp. 17–40. New Jersey: Lawrence Erlbaum.

Grossman, J. L. (1994). Women's Jury Service: Right of Citizenship or Privilege of Difference? *Stanford Law Review*, 46(5), 1115–60.

Hofer, P. (2000). Federal Sentencing for Violent and Drug Trafficking Crimes Involving Firearms: Recent Changes and Prospects for Improvement. *American Criminal Law Review* 37(4), 41–73.

Inciardi, J. A. (2000). *Criminal Justice*, 7th ed. Fort Worth, TX: Harcourt College Publishers.

Johnson, B. D. (2005). Contextual Disparities in Guideline Departures: Courtroom Social Contexts, Guideline Compliance, and Extralegal Disparities in Criminal Sentencing. *Criminology* 43(3), 761–98.

Kautt, P. & Spohn, C. (2002). Cracking Down on Black Drug Offenders? Testing for Interactions Among Offenders' Race, Drug Type, and Sentencing Strategy in Federal Drug Sentences. *Justice Quarterly* 19(1), 1–35.

Lieberman, J. D. (2011). The Utility of Scientific Jury Selection: Still Murky After 30 Years. *Current Directions in Psychological Science*, 20, 48–52.

Loftin, C., Heumann, M., & McDowall, D. (1983). Mandatory Sentencing and Firearms Violence: Evaluating an Alternative to Gun Control. *Law and Society Review* 17, 287–318.

Lowe, F. H. (2012). Black incarceration rates remain high, but prison rates drop overall. *Northstar News and Analysis*. Available online http://www.thenorthstarnews.com/Story/Black-Incarceration-Rates-Remain-High-but-Overall-Prison-Population-Drops

Mahoney, A. R.. (1982). American Jury Voir Dire and the Ideal of Equal Justice. *Journal of Applied Behavioral Science*, 18, 481–94.

Mauer, M., Potler, C., & Wolf, R. (2000). The impact of drug war on women: A comparative analysis in three states. *Women, Girls and Criminal Justice* 1(2), 21–22, 30–31.

McCoy, C. (1993). *Politics and Plea Bargaining: Victim's Rights in California*. Philadelphia: University of Philadelphia Press.

Miller, J. L. & Sloan J. (1994). A Study of Criminal Justice Discretion. *Journal of Criminal Justice* 22(2), 107–23.

Minnebo J. & Eggermont, S. (2007). Watching the young use illicit drugs: Direct experience, exposure to television and the stereotyping of adolescents' substance use. *Young, Nordic Journal of Youth Research*, 15(2), 129–44.

Morgan, M., & N. Signorielli. (1990). Cultivation Analysis: Conceptualization and

Methodology, in Nancy Signorielli and Michael Morgan (eds.), *Cultivation Analysis: New*

Directions in Media Effects Research, pp. 13–34. Newbury Park, CA: Sage.

Nellis, Ashley (2011). Policies and Practices That Contribute to Racial and Ethnic Disparity in Juvenile Justice. In Nicolle Parsons-Pollard (ed.), *Disproportionate Minority Contact: Current Issues and Policies*, pp. 3–14. Durham, NC: Carolina Academic Press.

Neubauer, D. W. (2005). *America's Courts and the Criminal Justice System*, 8th ed. Belmont, CA: Thomas Wadsworth.

Pollock, J. M. (2002). *Women, Prison and Crime*, 2nd ed. Belmont, CA: Wadsworth.

Poole, E. D. & Regoli, R. H. (1983). The Decision to Prosecute in Felony Cases. *Journal of Contemporary Criminal Justice* 2, 18–21.

Raeder, M. (1993a) Gender issues in the federal sentencing guidelines. *Journal of Criminal Justice*, 8(3), 20–35.

Raeder, M. (1993b). Gender and sentencing; single moms, battered women and other sex-based anomalies in the gender- free world of federal sentencing guidelines. *Pepperdine Law Review* 20(3), 905–90.

Remington, F. J., Kimball, E. L., Dickey, W. J., Goldstein, H., & Newman, D. J. (1981). *Criminal Justice Administration*. Indianapolis: Bobbs-Merrill.

Rose, D., & Clear, T. (1998). Incarceration, Social Capital, and Crime: Implications for Social Disorganization. *Criminology* 36(3),441–81.

Rosett, A. & Cressey, D. R. (1976). *Justice by Consent: Plea Bargains in the American Courthouse*. Philadelphia: Lippincott.

Smith, D. A. (1986). The Plea Bargaining Controversy. *Journal of Criminal Law and Criminology* 77(3), 949–68.

Sommers, S. R. & Norton, M. I. (2007). Race-based judgments, race-neutral justifications: Experimental examination of peremptory use and the Batson Challenge Procedure. *Law and Human Behavior*, 31(3), 261–73.

Spohn, C. (2000). Thirty years of sentencing reform: The quest for a racially neutral sentencing process. *Criminal Justice: The National Institute of Justice Journal*, 3, 427–501.

Spohn, C. & DeLone, M. (2000). When does race matter? An analysis of the conditions under which race affects sentence severity. *Sociology of Crime, Law, and Deviance*, 2, 3–37.

Steffensmeier, D., & Demuth, S. (2000). Ethnicity and sentencing outcomes in U.S. federal courts: Who is Punished More Harshly? *American Sociological Review*, 65, 705–29.

Steffensmeier, D., & Demuth, S. (2001). Ethnicity and Judges' Sentencing Decisions: Hispanic-Black-White Comparisons. *Criminology*, 39, 145–78.

Steffensmeier, D., Ulmer, J. T., & Kramer, J. (1998). The interaction of race, gender, and age in criminal sentencing: The punishment cost of being young, black, and male. *Criminology*, 36, 763–98.

The Sentencing Project (2007). *Women in the criminal justice system: Briefing sheets.* Available online at http://www.sentencingproject.org/doc/publications/womenincj_total.pdf

Tonry, M.. (1992). Mandatory Penalties. In Michael Tonry (ed.), *Crime and Justice: A Review of Research*, vol. 16, pp. 243–73. Chicago: University of Chicago Press.

Ulmer, J. T., Kurlychek, M. C., & Kramer, J. H. (2007). Prosecutorial discretion and the imposition of mandatory minimum sentences. *Journal of Research in Crime and Delinquency*, 44, 427–60.

Ulmer, J. T., &. Kramer, J. H. (1996). Court communities under sentencing guidelines: Dilemmas of formal rationality and sentencing disparity. *Criminology*, 34(3), 306–32.

Unner, J. D. and Gabbidon, S. L. (2011). *A Theory of African American Offending: Race, Racism and Crime*. New York: Routledge.

U.S. Sentencing Commission. (1991). The Federal Sentencing Guidelines: A Report on the Operation of the Guidelines System and Short-Term Impacts on Disparity in Sentencing, Use of Incarceration, and Prosecutorial Discretion and Plea Bargaining. Washington, DC.

van Wormer, K. & Bartollas, C. (2007). Women and the criminal justice system, 2nd ed. Boston: Allyn and Bacon.

Vogel, M. E. (1999). The social origins of plea bargaining: Conflict and the law in the process of state formation, 1830–1860. Law and Society Review, 33: 216–46.

Vorenberg, James. (2009). The Problem with Plea Bargaining: Differential Subjective Decision Making as an Engine of Racial Stratification in the United States Prison System. (Unpublished doctoral dissertation). Cornell University, Ithaca, NY. Retrieved from http://hdl.handle.net/1813/13836

Vorenberg, James. (1981). Decent restraint of prosecutorial power. Harvard Law Review, 94(7), 1521–73.

Walton, I. N. (2011). The prison industrial complex: Contributing mechanisms and collateral consequences of disproportionality on African-American communities. In Nicolle Parsons-Pollard (ed.), Disproportionate Minority Contact: Current Issues and Policies, pp. 215–33. Durham, NC: Carolina Academic Press.

Zatz, M. .(2000). The convergence of race, ethnicity, gender, and class on court decision making: Looking toward the 21st century. Criminal Justice: National Institute of Justice Journal, 3, 503–52.

Learn More on the Internet

Plea & Charge Bargaining: A Research Summary:
    http://www.ojp.gov/BJA/pdf/PleaBargainingResearchSummary.pdf
Frontline: The Plea:
    http://www.pbs.org/wgbh/pages/frontline/shows/plea/
Families Against Mandatory Minimums (FAMM):
    http://www.famm.org/

Discussion Questions

1. What are some of the ethical dilemmas that arise due to plea bargaining? Are these ethical dilemmas worth the trade-off of making the system more efficient?

2. Should prosecutors be allowed to retain the amount of discretion they have? Why or why not?

SECTION 4

RACE, GENDER, AND CORRECTIONS

CHAPTER SEVEN

Justice, War, and the Incarceration Boom

By Cheryl Lero Jonson

Introduction

In the 1960s and 1970s, Presidents Johnson and Nixon dramatically changed the course of U.S. penal history by declaring a **War on Crime** and a **War on Drugs**. The fundamental basis of these wars was that the crime and drug problem could be resolved if America made a commitment to "get tough" on these issues. This meant that the U.S. had to stop "coddling" criminals and focusing on the rehabilitation of offenders and, instead, replace this lenient treatment with harsh and severe sanctions (Clear, 1994; Garland, 2001). The main avenue in which to exact such severe punishment on offenders was to impose long and severe prison sentences on those who violated the law. Thus, prisons transformed from a sanction of last resort used only to punish the most heinous of offenders to the lynchpin of multiple correctional policies designed to deter both current and future offenders (Clear, 1994; Currie, 1998; Lynch, 2007; Zimring, 2001).

As a result of the "get tough" ideals underlying these two wars, various correctional and crime control policies were created, which resulted in dramatic increases in the prison population over the past four decades. These policies not only helped the United States earn the distinction of being the world's largest incarcerator, but they also were particularly detrimental to women and persons of color. However, due to the current budget crises, various states are retracting some of these harsh sanctions and moving back to a more rehabilitative or treatment-oriented vision of corrections in order to save money and reduce their prison populations.

"Get Tough" Policies and the Growth of America's Incarcerated Population

Under the guise that placing offenders behind bars would increase public safety, many tough-on-crime policies were created in order to guarantee that offenders would indeed be sentenced to prison. These policies included mandatory minimum sentences, three-strikes laws, and truth-in-sentencing legislation, which increased the likelihood that offenders would not only receive a prison sentence, but also would remain incarcerated for a long period of time. These policies accomplished their goal of sending and keeping people in prison; however, this harsh treatment of offenders contributed to the explosion of the American prison population.

Mandatory minimum sentencing policies require that individuals convicted of a certain crime be given a specific prison sentence (Sorenson and Stemen, 2002). There are multiple examples of these laws, but they are particularly associated with drug crimes. For example, Delaware passed their famous "three will get you three" law, in which possession of three grams of a controlled substance earned an individual three years in prison (Clear, 2007). In an analysis of sentencing policies from 1975–2002, Stemen, Rengifo, and Wilson (2005) discovered that mandatory minimum sentences for drug crimes had increased dramatically over the past quarter century. Particularly when examining the possession of one ounce of cocaine, Stemen and his associates found that the mandatory minimum sentence increased from 13 months in prison in 1975 to 28 months in 2002. A similar increase was also found when examining the sale of one ounce of cocaine, with sentences increasing from 25 months in 1975 to 41 months in 2002. Even more telling, Stemen et al. found similar results for multiple drug offenses, including the sale and possession of heroin, methamphetamine, and marijuana. Consequently, the **statutory sentences** related particularly to drug offenses resulted in large numbers of low-level dealers and users being incarcerated for long periods since the initiation of the Wars on Crime and Drugs.

Another **"get tough" policy** that impacted corrections was the movement toward repeat offender laws. **Three-strikes**, or **habitual offender**, **laws** quickly spread across the United States after the heinous killings of Kimber Reynolds and Polly Klaas by repeat, violent offenders (Schiraldi, Colburn, and Lotke, 2004; Tonry, 2004). These laws call for long prison terms, sometimes up to life imprisonment, for those who repeatedly violate the law. For example, in California, where the harshest of the three-strikes laws have been enacted, an offender will receive a life sentence without the possibly of parole for 25 years after a conviction of a third felony if the individual has been previously convicted of any violent felony (Stemen et al., 2005). Further, in California, offenders are sentenced to double the prison sentence if convicted of a second-strike offense. As of 2009, 28 states currently had some form of three-strikes laws on the books. This legislation seeks to "get tough" on repeat offender by imposing lengthy, mandatory prison terms for those who violate the law on multiple occasions.

A final tough-on-crime policy that was born out of the War on Crime and the War on Drugs was truth-in-sentencing legislation or laws imposing time-served requirements. **Truth-in-sentencing policies** had been adopted by 28 states by 2002 (Sabol, Rosich, Kane, Kirk, and Dubin, 2002; Stemen et al., 2005). These laws often required that an offender must serve a significant portion, often 85 percent, of their sentence before they would be eligible to be released from prison. In fact, three states—Wisconsin, Ohio, and North Carolina—required an offender to serve a full 100 percent of their sentence, prohibiting the chance of any type of early release (Stemen et al., 2005). The purpose of these laws was to ensure the time served by inmates closely matched the sentence that they were given by the court (Sorenson and Stemen, 2002). Consequently, many "back door" policies that would allow the early release of offenders were abolished. This, in combination with three-strikes laws and mandatory sentences, contributed to the dramatic increase in the prison populations seen during the War on Crime and the War on Drugs.

The Wars on Crime and Drugs and their subsequent reliance on **mass incarceration** through the above get-tough policies to solve the crime problem have resulted in the American prison population ballooning in size over the last four decades. In the 1970s, the state and federal prison populations were under 200,000 inmates (Blumstein and Beck, 1999). However, the following 40 years saw prison populations increase 600 percent, with currently over 1.6 million inmates housed in state and federal institutions on any given day. When current local jail populations are added, the number of U.S. citizens living behind bars on any given day climbs to over 2.4 million (Sabol, West, and Cooper, 2009; World Prison Brief, 2009). To place this number into context, there are more people in prison and jail in the United States than work for Wal-Mart and McDonald's worldwide (Nellis and King, 2009; Pager, 2007).

However, raw numbers can be deceiving, as they do not take into account the population changes that have occurred in the United States over the last four decades. Even when factoring in the fluctuations of the U.S. population in the past 40 years, the **imprisonment rate** has increased exponentially. Between 1925 and 1973, the imprisonment rate was fairly stable, ranging from 80 to 110 per 100,000 people. However, after the declaration of the Wars on Crime and Drugs, the imprisonment rate increased dramatically (Lynch, 2007). Specifically, the rate of imprisonment of state and federal prisons ballooned from 113 per 100,000 people at the close of the 1970s to presently 509 per 100,000 people. Similarly, increases in local jail incarceration rates have been recorded. In 1985, the incarceration rate of local jails was 108 per 100,000 people (*Sourcebook of Criminal Justice Statistics*, 2008). Twenty-six years later, the rate has more than doubled to 258 per 100,000 people (Minton and Sabol, 2009). When combining the jail and state and federal prison incarceration rates, the United States has an incarceration rate of 760 per 100,000 people, which is the highest incarceration rate in the world.

We Are Number One: America as the World's Largest Jailer

With 2.4 million people behind bars, America has become the largest jailer in the world. Although a handful of other Western industrialized countries have seen increases in their imprisonment rates, the rate found in the United States significantly dwarfs those found in any other nation. Still, unlike the United States, other nations, such as those in the Scandinavian region and Canada, have had much stability in their imprisonment rates for the last four decades. This finding suggests that an extensive dependence on incarceration in the last half century has not been a worldwide phenomenon.

When examining both the raw numbers and imprisonment rates, it is clear that America incarcerates more of their citizens than any other country in the world. The United States imprisons roughly 750,000 more individuals than China and roughly 1.5 million more than Russia, the world's second largest jailer (World Prison Brief, 2009). When examining imprisonment rates, the United States still leads the world with 760 inmates per 100,000 people in the population, followed by Russia with a rate of 620 people incarcerated per 100,000 (Hartney, 2006). In Europe, the highest imprisonment rate is found in the Czech Republic with a rate of 210, followed by Spain with a rate of 164, and England and Wales with a rate of 154 (See Figure 1). All these rates are less than one third of the rate found in the United States.

The large discrepancy in the rate of incarceration between America and other countries still remains and is quite pronounced when comparing the United States to its North American counterparts. For instance, the America's rate of 760 significantly dwarfs the rates of 116 found in Canada and 208 in Mexico. Consequently, America has a rate that is between four and eight times that of its industrialized European and North American counterparts, and a rate that is roughly 24 times higher than those countries (e.g., India, Senegal, Nigeria) with the lowest imprisonment rates in the world (Hartney, 2006; World Prison Brief, 2009).

To really gain an understanding of the true extent of America's use of imprisonment compared to the rest of the world, one only needs to examine the percent of the world's incarcerated population located in the United States.

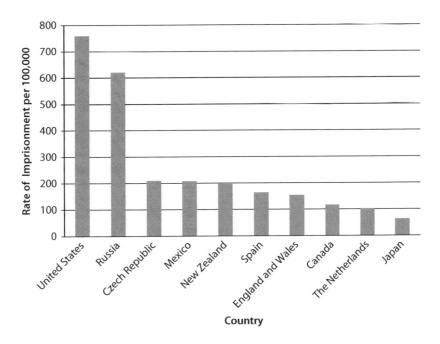

Figure 1: Worldwide Rates of Imprisonment per 100,000 Population

Although the United States accounts for only 5 percent of the world's population, it houses 25 percent of the over 9 million people incarcerated worldwide. Thus, one in four people incarcerated in the world is locked up in America (Warren, 2008). China, who has four times the population of the United States, only houses 14 percent of the world's incarcerated population. Notably, these two countries, China and the United States, have behind their bars roughly 40 percent of the world's imprisoned population, with the remaining 193 countries accounting for the other 60 percent.

Although America has shown a commitment to **mass imprisonment** for the past four decades, this has not been the case around the world (Tonry, 2007). Unlike America, the majority of the world's countries have not experienced a continuous increase in their imprisonment rate since the early 1970s (Tonry, 2007). Rather, the imprisonment rates around the world have varied widely, with some nations maintaining a stable rate, while others were decreasing, some only recently increasing, and still others having varying rates over the last four decades.

In Europe, the Scandinavian countries of Denmark, Norway, and Sweden have had stable imprisonment rates of between 40–60 prisoners per 100,000 population for the last half century (Lappi-Seppala, 2007). Germany has also had stable imprisonment rates for the last 25 years, hovering around 90 inmates per 100,000 population (Weigend, 2001). In contrast, the imprisonment rates in Finland actually decreased substantially from 1965 to 1990 and have stabilized since hovering around 65 inmates per 100,000 population (Lappi-Seppala, 2007; Tonry, 2007).

One particularly revealing international comparison is that between the United States and Canada. In his cross-cultural comparison, Brodeur (2007) demonstrated that countries that clustered together geographically and culturally seem to incarcerate people at roughly the same rate. Specifically, he found that within the five clusters (e.g., Nordic Council countries, Central European countries, the Baltic countries, the Caribbean, and the Indian subcontinent), the countries had remarkably similar imprisonment rates. The United States and Canada share one of the world's largest common borders, second only to the border shared between Russia and China (Brodeur, 2007). Due to this geographic proximity, one would expect Canada to be similar to the United States in terms of their incarceration rates (Brodeur, 2007). However, this is not the case. While the U.S. incarceration rate has greatly increased since the 1970s, the rate in Canada has remained relatively stable at around 100 inmates per 100,000 population since the 1960s (Ouimet, 2002; Webster and Doob, 2007). Despite the cultural, economic, and geographical similarities between the two countries, America's rate of imprisonment is 6.5 times higher than that of Canada (World Prison Brief, 2009), thus illuminating the United States' unique reliance on imprisonment in response to criminal behavior.

Although many countries have had stable or decreasing rates, America is not alone among countries that have shown an increase in the use of imprisonment. However, what is distinct about the United States is the length and the enormity of that expansion. For example, England and Wales and New Zealand have shown substantial increases in their imprisonment rates; however, this has only occurred since the 1990s (Newburn, 2007; Pratt, 2007; Tonry, 2007). Similarly, Japan has shown a recent increase in the use of incarceration. After approximately three decades of falling or stable prison populations, the number of inmates in Japan increased 15 percent between 1990 and 2005 (Johnson, 2007). However, in spite of the increased use of imprisonment in these nations, their imprisonment rates are still substantially lower than that of the United States. For instance, as of 2009, England and Wales have an imprisonment rate of 154, New Zealand has a rate of 197, and Japan has a rate of 63 inmates per 100,000 population (See Figure 1) (World Prison Brief, 2009). Despite the recent expansion in the use of imprisonment in these countries, the United States still has an incarceration rate roughly four to 12 times higher than these nations.

Out of 195 countries in the world, only one other nation besides the United States—the Netherlands—has seen a constantly increasing imprisonment rate for roughly the past 40 years (Downes, 2007; Tonry, 2007). However, it is important to note that although the Netherlands has experienced a seven-fold increase in their incarceration rate since 1973, the result of this 38-year expansion has not corresponded to an exceptionally high imprisonment rate (100 per 100,000 population) (Tonry, 2007; World Prison Brief, 2009). Thus, when all the international statistics are compared, it becomes apparent that the willingness of countries to place a substantial number of their citizens behind bars is not a worldwide phenomenon; rather, this is a case of **American exceptionalism**.

The War on Women

The Wars on Crime and Drugs have dramatically increased the numbers of people behind bars. However, these "get tough" campaigns have had a particularly detrimental impact on women. In fact, the number of women imprisoned in the United States has increased substantially since 1977, rising from roughly 11,000 women incarcerated to currently over 198,000 women behind bars (Glaze, 2010; Greene and Pranis, 2006). When examining rates, this rise becomes even more pronounced. In 1973, the imprisonment rate for women was just 6 per 100,000 people. In 30 years, this rose to 64 per 100,000 by 2004, corresponding to an increase of over 965 percent (Lynch, 2007).

This explosion of women serving time in prisons and jails has been driven primarily by the increased number of women being incarcerated for low-level, nonviolent and drug offenses (Mauer and King, 2007). In fact, 43 percent of the increase in women's incarceration has been due to drug offenses, as opposed to 28 percent of the growth of men's incarceration (Blumstein and Beck, 1999). When examining the offense types of males and females in state and federal prisons, it becomes exceptionally clear that women are more often sentenced and confined in prisons for minor offenses compared to their male counterparts. In 2006, more than half (53.4 percent) of males were sentenced to state or federal prison for violent offenses compared to only 34.0 percent of females. On the other hand, two thirds of women in prison were incarcerated for nonviolent offenses, with over one quarter convicted solely of a drug offense (Sabol, Couture, and Harrison, 2007).

Not only has the War on Drugs increased the overall rate of imprisonment for women, but its impact has been particularly burdensome on women of color. In 2008, one in every 265 women between the ages of 35–39 was incarcerated. When this number was broken down by race, it becomes apparent that minority women have faced the brunt of this imprisonment binge, with one in 355 white women, one in 297 Hispanic women, and one in 100 black women incarcerated in the United States (Warren, 2008). Black women, who only constitute 12 percent of the female population, make up more than 50 percent of the U.S. female prison population (Sokoloff, 2005).

Even more telling are the lifetime chances of women going to prison. In 1973, a woman had a 0.3 percent chance of serving time behind bars. By 2001, the lifetime chances of a woman going to prison increased sixfold to 1.8 percent. When examining these chances by race, it becomes apparent that minority women are especially more likely to be involved in the correctional system. Of black women born in 2001, 5.6 percent are expected to enter prison in their lifetime, whereas only 2.2 percent of Hispanic women and 0.9 percent white females are expected to serve time in a state or federal prison during their lifetime (Bonczar, 2003; Currie, 1998; Mauer and King, 2007).

When specifically examining the impact of drug offenses on women of color, it becomes apparent that minority women have been particularly affected by the War on Drugs. In five short years (1986–1991), the number of white women incarcerated for drug offenses increased 241 percent (Mauer and Huling, 2005). Although this number is exceptionally high, it is dwarfed when compared to the increase seen for black and Hispanic women. Hispanic women's incarceration rates for the same five years increased 328 percent, while the incarceration rate for black women rose an astonishing 828 percent in five years (Mauer and Huling, 2005). Consequently, women—particularly minority women—have felt the brunt of the War on Drugs.

This increase in the number of women incarcerated presents unique challenges. As 70–80 percent of women in prison have children, their incarceration can be detrimental not only to themselves but also to the children they are leaving behind (Jacobs, 2000). As female institutions are fewer in number than male institutions, women offenders are often placed in facilities that are much further from their families. Thus, female inmates often receive fewer visits than their male counterparts, increasing the hardship on mothers who are incarcerated (Chesney-Lind, 2004). In fact, more than half of the female inmate population will receive absolutely no visits from their children while behind bars (Chesney-Lind, 2004).

Although the majority of women (80 percent) plan to be reunited with their children upon release, there are many challenges that await these women when they walk out of the prison gates (Greene and Pranis, 2006). These women may have their parental rights terminated while incarcerated if the child is placed in foster care for 15 of the last 22 months, in accordance with the Adoption and Safe Families Act of 1997. Thus, if they are trying to keep their family intact, they have to develop strategies on how to keep their children out of foster care while imprisoned (Jacobs, 2000).

Furthermore, many newly released women may have a difficult time providing for their families once leaving the prison walls. It is well documented that having a felony conviction decreases the chances of obtaining employment (Pager, 2007). Additionally, with the recent changes to welfare benefits (e.g., food stamps and housing assistance), it becomes exceedingly difficult not only for a women released from prison to find a home and afford life's necessities for herself, but also to provide for her family (Jacobs, 2000). Consequently, not only does the woman suffer, but so do her children.

The War on Drugs, although intended to increase public safety and the quality of life for the public, has not achieved its desired goal. Rather, this war has been an attack mainly on the minority community. As Clear (2007) explains, this over-incarceration of minorities has made "disadvantaged neighborhoods worse" by reducing the informal social control present. Minority communities are losing many of its members to this war and, in turn, children are losing parents, role models, and social capital. This war then has had the latent consequence of perpetuating a **cycle of disadvantage** in these minority communities, rather than alleviating the problem it had intended to solve.

The War on Minorities

Although the raw numbers and rates of people incarcerated in the United States presented above are at unprecedented levels, there is a differential use of imprisonment among the races, both among men and women, in America. The research examining the disproportionate use of imprisonment between minority and white Americans dates back from the early 1980s, with both the older and more recent research reaching a similar conclusion: African Americans, and more recently Hispanics, are incarcerated at a higher rate than whites (Abramsky, 2002; Beckett and Western, 2001; Blumstein, 1982, 1993; Garland, Spohn, and Wodahl, 2008; Jacobs and Carmichael, 2001; Lynch, 2007; Mauer, 1999; Miller, 1996; Parenti, 2000; Tonry, 1995; Wacquant 2000, 2001, 2002). In raw numbers, roughly 900,000 of the 1.6 million current prisoners in the United States are African American or Hispanic (Mauer and King, 2007; Sabol et al., 2009).

One way to examine **racial disparity** in imprisonment is to compare the percentages of minorities in the general population to the percent that are incarcerated (Lynch, 2007). Although African Americans make up 12 percent of the U.S. population, they constitute 38 percent of the prison population. Hispanics are also overrepresented, comprising 15 percent of the U.S. population but 20 percent of the prison population. While both blacks and Hispanics are severely overrepresented in the prison system, their white counterparts are substantially underrepresented. The U.S. population is 69 percent white, but the prison population is only 34 percent white (Human Rights Watch, 2002, 2003; Lynch, 2007; Sabol et al., 2009). Although minorities have in recent times significantly outnumbered whites in prison, this has not always been the case. As early as 40 years ago, 70 percent of the prison population was white. This has drastically reversed in four short decades, with now roughly 60 percent of the prison population black or Hispanic (Gottschalk, 2006; Sabol et al., 2009; Wacquant, 2001).

It is thus well established that there are substantial differences in the incarceration rates of whites, blacks, and Hispanics, and there has been much research examining the reason for this racial difference. Many commentators have argued that the reason for this disparity is the **differential offending rates** of the races and the increased enforcement of drug crimes in recent decades (Blumstein, 1993; Garland et al., 2008; Gottschalk, 2006; Human Rights Watch, 2002, 2003; Mauer, 1999; Wacquant, 2001; Weich and Angulo, 2000; Ziedenberg and Schiraldi, 2005). Before the launch of the War on Drugs, researchers found evidence that the racial differences in prison were primarily due to the differential offending rates of whites and blacks. For example, in his landmark study, Blumstein (1982) discovered that 80 percent of the racial discrepancy in state prisons could be explained by the racial disproportionality in offending. Specifically, he found that although blacks constituted 49 percent of the state prison population in 1979, they also comprised 43 percent of the arrests for that year. Thus, he concluded that the offending rates of blacks is what drives their higher incarceration rate rather than racially discriminating practices.

Blumstein's (1982) findings were confirmed by two other studies. First, Langan (1985) demonstrated that roughly 85 percent of the racial disparity in state prison admissions could be explained by racial differences in offending. Second, Blumstein replicated his 1982 study in 1993. Examining crime generally, Blumstein confirmed his earlier findings by showing that 74 percent of the racial disparities in prison could be explained by differential offending rates.

However, more recently, Tonry and Melewski (2008) did not fully reproduce Blumstein's earlier findings. Tonry and Melewski discovered that the amount of disparity in prison explained by differential offending patterns by whites and blacks has decreased substantially in the past 20 years. Whereas Blumstein found that 80 percent of the racial disparity was explained by differences in offending, Tonry and Melewski determined that only 61 percent could now be explained by blacks' greater involvement in crime. Consequently, roughly 40 percent of the racial disparity in imprisonment was *not* explained by differences in offending.

Most telling, the findings showing that much disparity could be explained by differential offending rates particularly did not hold when examining drug offenses. Notably, one of the earliest studies to discover this discrepancy concerning drug offenses was conducted by Blumstein. In both of his 1982 and 1993 articles, he decided to not only examine crime in general but also specific types of crime. When examining drug offenses, he found that only 50 percent (as opposed to the roughly 75 percent for crime in general) of the racial disparity in state prisons could be explained by offending rates. Even more striking is that when Blumstein excluded the drug offenses from his analysis, over 90 percent of the disparity in incarceration was explained by differential offending. Consequently, for drug offenses, Blumstein concluded that there was some level of discrimination or differential enforcement occurring between whites and blacks.

More recently, substantial differences in the incarceration rates for drug offenses among whites and minorities have been documented. Nationally, blacks and Hispanics are sent to prison for drug offenses at a much higher rate than whites (Blumstein, 1982; 1993; Crutchfield et al., 1994; Human Rights Watch, 2000, 2002; Mauer, 1999, 2009; Langan 1985; Lynch, 2007; Sampson and Lauritsen, 1997; Tonry, 1995; Tonry and Melewski, 2008). In Mauer's (2009) testimony to the Subcommittee on Crime, Terrorism, and Homeland Security, he presented evidence for this racial disparity. He argued that although blacks constitute 14 percent of current illicit drug users, they comprise roughly 34 percent of drug arrests and 53 percent of people sentenced to prison for drug offenses. Thus, blacks are, in fact, being targeted and treated more harshly than their white counterparts for drug crimes. Mauer suggested two ways in which blacks are disproportionately targeted: federal crack cocaine laws of the 1980s and school zone drug laws that disproportionately target minorities (Mauer, 2009). Although it may not be outright, overt **discrimination** among the police, courts, and lawmakers, it is possible that there is racial discrimination covertly written into and produced by U.S. drug laws.

Texas is one state in which the differential impact of the War on Drugs is especially pronounced. Ziedenberg and Schiraldi (2005) report that in Texas, the number of African Americans incarcerated for drug offenses increased 360 percent between 1986 to 1999, while the number of whites imprisoned for drug offenses decreased by 9 percent in that same time period. What is remarkable about this is just not the vast difference between blacks and whites, but that national studies have shown that whites and blacks use illicit drugs at a similar rate (8.5 percent versus 9.7 percent, respectively) (Substance Abuse and Mental Health Services Administration, 2003). Consequently, Ziedenberg and Schiraldi argue that blacks are disproportionately being targeted by the War on Drugs and are arrested and imprisoned at higher rates for their drug use than their white counterparts.

This over-incarceration of minorities has serious and detrimental impacts on the minority population. Incarceration has long lasting impacts after the individual leaves the prison gates (Austin and Irwin, 2001). Once a person is "marked" as a convict, people often begin to view this person as suspicious and untrustworthy. Friends and family often no longer associate with the individual, leaving the person to associate with other antisocial individuals (Sampson and Laub, 1993). It also becomes very difficult for these individuals to obtain work, as many employers are reluctant to hire ex convicts (Holzer, 2007; Holzer, Raphael, and Stoll, 2004, 2006, 2007; Pager, 2003, 2007). Further, in several states, ex prisoners lose the right to vote and many opportunities to participate in civil society (Abramsky, 2006; Fellner and Mauer, 1998). Faced with a lack of positive associates and employment and an inability to participate in civil society, these individuals often find themselves in highly criminogenic situations once outside the prison walls. Because of the overrepresentation of minorities in prison, these problems disproportionately affect blacks and Hispanics. Consequently, the impact of the Wars on Drugs and Crime become social justice issues, as its effects are largely concentrated among minorities in the United States.

Rethinking "Get Tough" to Save Money

In light of budget crises, many states have begun to rethink their "get tough" on crime policies. As of 2009, the 50 states spend over $52 billion annually in corrections costs. This corresponds to one out of every 15 state general discretionary dollars, or 6.8 percent of states' general funds, being spent on the correctional enterprise (Pew Center on the States, 2009; Warren, 2008). When specifically examining the costs of housing a *single* individual in an institution, a state spends, on average, $79 per day, or approximately $29,000 annually (Pew Center on the States, 2009). Thus, an exceptional amount of money is expended on the imprisonment of people, and this expenditure has increased over the past four decades due to the Wars on Crime and Drugs.

In an effort to save money, many states have enacted legislation to reduce their prison populations. Some of these efforts have sought to release nonviolent or drug offenders, while others have attempted to sentence fewer offenders to prison or jail. Regardless, a movement away from "get tough" policies is beginning to be seen across the nation.

One example of these more lenient policies is **Kentucky's House Bill 463**. This law, which was signed by Governor Beshear in 2011, seeks to impose "presumptive probation," rather than a prison term, on low-level drug offenders, while increasing penalties for large-scale trafficking violations. Further, the law requires community-based drug treatment to be offered to offenders convicted of low-level drug offenses. Additionally, HB 463 reduces the sentences associated with small-time drug dealing, lowering the sale of small amounts of many controlled substances from a Class C felony to a Class D felony. Finally, the law allows there to be **graduated sanctions** for those offenders found in violation of their probation or parole, further reducing the number of people who would be returned to prison for technical violations (ACLU, 2011).

New York provides another example of a state retracting some of the tough-on-crime policies passed under the Wars on Crime and Drugs. In 2004, New York passed the **Drug Reform Act**. This act reduced the mandatory minimum sentence associated for a first-time class A-1 drug offense from 15 to eight years. It additionally doubled the amount or weight of the controlled substance needed to receive the mandatory sentence (New York State Department of Correctional Services, 2004).

In June 2011, Ohio also signed prison reform legislation that both reduced sentences associated with drug crimes and nonviolent offenses. Specifically, **HB 86** reduced the mandatory minimum sentences associated with marijuana offenses. Additionally, in order for a property crime to be classified as a felony, the monetary value must reach $1000 instead of $500. Furthermore, the law requires that **alternatives to incarceration** must be given for low-level felonies and misdemeanors. Finally, to reduce the population of those already incarcerated, HB 86 increased **parole eligibility** and earned credit programs for offenders (ACLU, 2011).

The above are just a few examples of the various states passing "smarter sentencing" strategies for low-level nonviolent offenders (ACLU, 2011). Although fueled by monetary concerns, the "get tough" policies that were the basis of the Wars on Crime and Drugs are beginning to fracture. The days of imposing harsh, mandatory sentences with little or no possibility of parole are quickly vanishing. Instead, sentences that focus on the rehabilitation of offenders in the community are beginning to take hold and spread across the country, with the hopes of reducing—rather than increasing—the number of people placed behind prison bars.

Conclusion

In closing, the Wars on Crime and Drugs have dramatically changed the penal landscape of the United States. The public perception of criminals as wayward individuals who needed to be "corrected" was dramatically altered and replaced with an image of individuals who were seen as rational beings that chose to commit crime and thus deserved to be punished with long and severe sanctions. This belief that offenders deserve harsh punishment bore various "get tough" policies that have had dramatic impacts on America's penal population, making America a nation that had become "addicted to incarceration" (Pratt, 2009). This addiction has had especially detrimental impacts on women and minorities. However, although not due to changes in ideals, this addiction is slowly being "cured." With various states in budget crises, a movement back to the treatment and rehabilitation of offenders has begun. With luck, policy makers and the public will see that these programs can be effective in changing the law violating to law abiding and will continue in this direction when the recession is over. Hopefully, then, the United States will be able to cure its own addiction to imprisonment, especially among women and persons of color.

References

Abramsky, S. (2006). *Conned: How millions went to prison, lost the vote, and helped send George W. Bush to the White House.* New York: New Press.

ACLU. (2011). *Smart reform is possible: States reducing incarceration rates while protecting communities.* New York: American Civil Liberties Union.

Austin, J., & Irwin, J. (2001). *It's about time: America's imprisonment binge,* 3rd ed. Belmont, CA: Wadsworth.

Beckett, K., & Western, B. (2001). Governing social marginality. In D. Garland (ed.), *Mass imprisonment: Social causes and consequences.* London: Sage Publications.

Blumstein, A. (1982). On racial disproportionality of the United States' prison populations. *Journal of Criminal Law and Criminology, 73,* 743-760.

Blumstein, A. (1993). Racial disproportionality of U.S. prison populations revisited. *University*

of Colorado Law Review, 64, 743–760.

Blumstein, A., & Beck, A. J. (1999). Population growth in U.S. prisons, 1980–1996. In M. Tonry & J. Petersilia (eds.), *Crime and Justice: A Review of the Research, vol. 26, Prisons* (pp. 17–61). Chicago: University of Chicago Press.

Bonczar, T. (2003). *Prevalence of imprisonment in the U.S. population, 1974–2001.* Washington, DC: Bureau of Justice Statistics, U.S. Department of Justice.

Brodeur, J.-P. (2007). Comparative penology in perspective. In M. Tonry (ed.), *Crime and justice: A review of research* (vol. 36, Crime, punishment, and politics in comparative perspective, pp. 49–92). Chicago: University of Chicago Press.

Chesney-Lind, M. (2004). *The female offender: Girls, women and crime.* 2nd ed. Thousand Oaks, CA: Sage.

Clear, T. R. (1994). *Harm in American penology: Offenders, victims, and their communities.* Albany: State University of New York Press.

Clear, T. R. (2007). *Imprisoning communities: How mass incarceration makes disadvantaged neighborhoods worse.* New York: Oxford University Press.

Currie, E. (1998). *Crime and punishment in America.* New York: Metropolitan Books.

Downes, D. (2007). Visions of penal control in the Netherlands. In M. Tonry (ed.), *Crime and justice: A review of research* (vol. 36, Crime, punishment, and politics in comparative perspective, pp. 93–126). Chicago: University of Chicago Press.

Fellner, J. & Mauer, M. (1998). *Losing the vote: The impact of felony disenfranchisement laws in the United States.* Washington, DC: The Sentencing Project.

Garland, B., Spohn, C., & Wodahl, E. J. (2008). Racial disproportionality in the American prison population: Using the Blumstein method to address the critical race and justice issue of the 21st century. *Justice Policy Journal, 5*(2), 1–42.

Garland, D. (2001). *The culture of control: Crime and social order in contemporary society.* Chicago: University of Chicago Press.

Glaze, L. (2010). *Correctional populations in the United States, 2009.* Washington, DC: Bureau of Justice Statistics, U.S. Department of Justice.

Greene, J., & Pranis, K. (2006). *Hard hit: The growth and imprisonment of women, 1977–2004.* Washington, DC: Women's Prison Association.

Hartney, C. (2006). *U.S. rates of incarceration: A global perspective.* Oakland, CA: National Council on Crime and Delinquency.

Holzer, H. J. (2007). *Collateral costs: The effects of incarceration on employment and earnings among young men.* Madison, WI: Institute for Research on Poverty.

Holzer, H. J., Raphael, S., & Stoll, M. (2004). Will employers hire former offenders? Employer preference, background checks and their determinants. In M. Pattillo, D. Weiman, & B. Western (eds.), *Imprisoning America: The social effects of mass incarceration* (pp. 205–246). New York: Russell Sage.

Human Rights Watch. (2002). *Race and incarceration in the United States.* New York: Human Rights Watch.

Human Rights Watch. (2003). *Incarcerated America.* New York: Human Rights Watch.

Jacobs, A. (2000). Give 'em a fighting chance: The challenges for women offenders trying to succeed in the community. In *Topics in Community Corrections* (pp. 44–49). Washington, DC: National Institute of Justice.

Jacobs, D., & Carmichael, J. T. (2001). The politics of punishment across time and space: A pooled time-series analysis of imprisonment rates. *Social Forces, 80,* 61–89.

Johnson, D. T. (2007). Crime and punishment in contemporary Japan. In M. Tonry (ed.), *Crime and justice: A review of research* (vol. 36, Crime, punishment, and politics in comparative perspective, pp. 371–424). Chicago: University of Chicago Press.

Langan, P. (1985). Racism on trial: New evidence to explain the racial composition of prisons in the United States. *Journal of Criminal Law and Criminology, 76,* 666–683.

Lappi-Seppala, T. (2007). Penal policies in Scandinavia. In M. Tonry (ed.), *Crime and justice: A review of research* (vol. 36, Crime, punishment, and politics in comparative perspective, pp. 217–296). Chicago: University of Chicago Press.

Lynch, M. J. (2007). *Big prisons, big dreams: Crime and the failure of America's penal system.* New Brunswick, NJ: Rutgers University Press.

Mauer, M. (1999). *Race to incarcerate.* New York: New Press.

Mauer, M. (2009). *Racial disparities in the criminal justice system: Prepared for the House Judiciary Subcommittee on Crime, Terrorism, and Homeland Security.* Washington, DC: The Sentencing Project.

Mauer, M., & Huling T. (2007). *Young black Americans and the criminal justice system: Five years later.* Washington, DC: The Sentencing Project.

Mauer, M., & King, R. S. (2007). *A 25-year quagmire: The War on Drugs and its impact on American society.* Washington, DC: The Sentencing Project.

Minton, T. D., & Sabol, W. J. (2009). *Jail inmates at midyear 2008: Statistical tables.* Washington, DC: Bureau of Justice Statistics, U.S. Department of Justice.

Nellis, A., & King, R. S. (2009). *No exit: The expanding use of life sentences in America.* Washington, DC: The Sentencing Project.

New York State Department of Correctional Services. (2004). Pataki signs Rocky drug reform into law. *Docs Today, 13,* 4–5.

Newburn, T. (2007). "Tough on crime": Penal policy in England and Wales. In M. Tonry (ed.), *Crime and justice: A review of research* (vol. 36, Crime, punishment, and politics in comparative perspective, pp. 425–470). Chicago: University of Chicago Press.

Ouimet, M. (2002). Explaining the Canadian and American crime "drop" in the 1990s. *Canadian Journal of Criminology, 44,* 33–50.

Pager, D. (2003). The mark of a criminal record. *American Journal of Sociology, 108,* 937–975.

Pager, D. (2007). *Marked: Race, crime, and finding work in an era of mass incarceration.* Chicago: University of Chicago Press.

Pew Center on the States. (2009). *One in 31: The Long Reach of American Corrections.* Washington, DC: The Pew Charitable Trusts.

Pratt, T. (2009). *Addicted to incarceration: Corrections policy and the politics of misinformation in the United States.* Thousand Oaks, CA: Sage.

Sabol, W. J., Couture, H., & Harrison, P. M. (2007). *Prisoners in 2006.* Washington, DC: Bureau of Justice Statistics, U.S. Department of Justice.

Sabol, W. J., Rosich, K., Kane, K. M., Kirk, D., & Dubin, G. (2002). *Influences of truth-in-sentencing reform changes in states' sentencing practices and prison populations.* Washington, DC: U.S. Department of Justice

Sabol, W. J., West, H. C., & Cooper, M. (2009). *Prisoners in 2008.* Washington, DC: Bureau of Justice Statistics, U.S. Department of Justice.

Sampson, R. J., & Laub, J. H. (1993). *Crime in the making: Pathways and turning points through life.* Cambridge, MA: Harvard University Press.

Schiraldi, V., Colburn, J., & Lotke, E. (2004). Three strikes and you're out: An examination of the impact of strikes laws 10 years after their enactment. Washington, DC: Justice Policy Institute.

Sokoloff, N. (2005). Women prisoners at the dawn of the 20th century. *Women in Criminal Justice, 16,* 127–137.

Sorenson, J. & Stemen, D. (2002). The effect of state sentencing policies on incarceration rates. *Crime and Delinquency, 48,* 456–475.

Sourcebook of Criminal Justice Statistics. (2008). Washington, DC: Bureau of Justice Statistics, U.S. Department of Justice.

Stemen, D., Rengifo, A., & Wilson, J. (2005). *Of fragmentation and ferment: The impact of state sentencing policies on incarceration rates, 1975–2002.* Washington, DC: U.S. Department of Justice.

Substance Abuse and Mental Health Services Administration. (2003). *Results from the 2002 National Survey on Drug Use and Health: National Findings.* Rockville, MD: Office of Applied Studies, U.S. Department of Health and Human Services.

Tonry, M. (1995). *Malign neglect: Race, crime, and punishment in America.* New York: Oxford University Press.

Tonry, M. H. (2004). *Thinking about crime: Sense and sensibility in American penal culture.* New York: Oxford University Press.

Tonry, M. (2007). Determinants of penal policies. In M. Tonry (ed.), *Crime and justice: A review of research* (vol. 36, Crime, punishment, and politics in comparative perspective, pp. 1–48). Chicago: University of Chicago Press.

Tonry, M., & Melewski, M. (2008). The malign effects of drug and crime control policies on black Americans. In M. Tonry (ed.), *Crime and justice: A review of research* (vol. 37, pp. 1–44). Chicago: University of Chicago Press.

Wacquant, L. (2000). The new "peculiar institution": On the prison as surrogate ghetto. *Theoretical Criminology, 4,* 377–389.

Wacquant, L. (2001). Deadly symbiosis: When ghetto and prison meet and mesh. *Punishment and Society, 3,* 95–134.

Warren, J. (2008). *One in 100: Behind bars in America.* Washington, DC: The Pew Charitable Trusts.

Webster, C. M., & Doob, A. N. (2007). Punitive trends and stable imprisonment rates in Canada. In M. Tonry (ed.), *Crime and justice: A review of research* (vol. 36, Crime, punishment, and politics in comparative perspective, pp. 297–370). Chicago: University of Chicago Press.

Weigend, T. (2001). Sentencing and punishment in Germany. In M. Tonry & R. S. Frase (eds.), *Sentencing and sanctions in western countries* (pp. 188–221). New York: Oxford University Press.

World Prison Brief. (2009). London: King's College London, International Centre for Prison Studies.

Ziedenberg, J., & Schiraldi, V. (2005). *Race and imprisonment in Texas: The disparate incarceration of Latinos and African Americans in the Lone Star State.* Washington, DC: Justice Policy Institute.

Zimring, F. (2001). Imprisonment rates and the new politics of criminal punishment. In D. Garland (ed.), *Mass imprisonment: Social causes and consequences* (pp. 145–149). Thousand Oaks, CA: Sage Publications.

Learn More on the Internet:

Correctional Populations in the United States:
http://bjs.ojp.usdoj.gov/index.cfm?ty=pbdetail&iid=2237

The Sentencing Project:
http://www.sentencingproject.org/template/index.cfm

Women's Prison Association:
  http://www.wpaonline.org/

Discussion Questions:

1. How did the United States get-tough-on-crime policies affect those of color, the poor, and/or females who became involved in the criminal justice system?
2. Why are states changing their get-tough-on-crime policies? Do you think this new line of thinking will increase or decrease crime rates?

CHAPTER EIGHT

Arbitrariness and Disparities in the Administration of the Death Penalty

By Diana Falco

Introduction

The use of the death penalty as a form of punishment in the United States is one of the most highly debated issues among American citizens, political officials, criminal justice professionals, and academic researchers. It is certainly considered a "hot topic," due to the fact that capital punishment is traditionally considered the most punitive form of punishment, particularly because of the finality and irreversibility of the sanction. In addition, because of the fact that the death penalty is irreversible, the importance of ensuring its fair application is high. Although capital punishment continues to be used in the United States, the debate over its use has not ended. Various issues related to arbitrariness (e.g., discrimination based on race, class, geography, etc.), innocence, cost, and deterrence have been highly debated.

Controversial death penalty cases often bring this debate to the forefront of media reports and political discussions. Recently, the execution of Troy Davis on September 21, 2011, in Georgia brought both the innocence and racial imbalance debates back into the spotlight. Troy Davis was convicted and executed for the murder of an off-duty police officer in 1989. The Davis case drew national attention due to serious doubts about his guilt after a number of eyewitnesses recanted their statements and a general lack of physical evidence in the case (Severson, 2011). Although Davis was eventually executed, his case garnered a great deal of support among abolitionists (including former president Jimmy Carter and Pope Benedict XVI) and many more who believe that politicians and the courts should reexamine the use of capital punishment in America.

Again, news reporters, politicians, and American citizens are discussing the use of the death penalty and their feelings about how it is applied. This chapter will discuss some of the issues surrounding the death penalty. First, it will discuss the history and extent of its use in the United States. Within this section, the author will report the rulings on a number of important Supreme Court cases. Next, it will discuss the issue of arbitrariness—specifically, how the death penalty may be capriciously applied based on geography, race, and social class. Last, the chapter will briefly discuss the extent and use of the death penalty around the world.

History and Use of the Death Penalty in the United States

Although this topic remains a hotly debated issue in modern times, the use of the death penalty as a punishment for wrongdoing has existed for centuries. The methods of administration have varied and include various forms of torture, beheading, hanging, death by firing squad, gas chamber, electrocution, and lethal injection. Its use remained popular in Europe prior to the colonization of America. Since the American system was based largely on the British model, the death penalty has been present throughout the history of the United States.

The use of the death penalty has continued, due primarily to the extent of public support for the sanction. Bohm (2003) argues that public support for the death penalty contributes to its continued use in at least five ways. First, strong public support can sway legislators to vote in favor of the death penalty and against any statutes seeking its repeal. Second, he argues that prosecutors may seek the death penalty for political rather than legal purposes. Third, it may influence judges to impose death sentences or uphold death sentences on appeal. Fourth, governors may be less likely to veto death penalty legislation or commute a death sentence due to fear of risking reelection. Lastly, and what Bohm argues is the most important, is that supreme court justices (both state and federal) examine support for the death penalty as a measure of "evolving standards of decency" to decide whether the death penalty violates the U.S. Constitution's Eighth Amendment "cruel and unusual punishment" clause.

Although the constitutionality of the death penalty had been questioned, it wasn't until the Supreme Court case *Furman v. Georgia* (1972) that capital punishment, as it was applied at the time, was found to violate the cruel and unusual punishment clause of the Eighth Amendment. However, this position did not last long, and four years later the Court ruled in *Gregg v. Georgia* (1976) that the death penalty was not inherently unconstitutional. To date, 1972–1976 remains the only time in U.S. history that the death penalty was not in practice.

Although the discourse on this subject remains strong since *Gregg*, capital punishment continues to be used as a form of punishment today. According to the Death Penalty Information Center (DPIC) (2011), there are 34 states with the death penalty (as well as the U.S. government and U.S. military) and 16 states without the death penalty. Since 1976, there have been 1,271 executions. Although its use continues, the number of executions has had a steady decline since 1999 (98 executions) as compared to 2010 (46 executions). Since 2007, four states have abolished the death penalty: New York, New Jersey, New Mexico, and Illinois. Whether or not the decline in number of death sentences or a decrease in the amount of states with the death penalty is an indicator of a general move toward abolition still remains in question.

Important Supreme Court Decisions since 1972

In 1972, the U.S. Supreme Court ruled in ***Furman v. Georgia*** that the death penalty, as administered at the time, violated the Eighth Amendment. The *Furman* case questioned whether the death penalty was arbitrarily and capriciously applied. The argument is that the death penalty would violate the Eighth Amendment's "cruel and unusual punishment" clause if the death penalty is not fairly applied across similar cases, offenders, and victims. In a 5 to 4 vote, with nine separate written decisions by Court justices, the Georgia statute was declared unconstitutional. In the concurring opinion, Justice Douglas suggested that "the high service rendered by the 'cruel and unusual' punishment clause of the Eighth Amendment is to require legislatures to write penal laws that are evenhanded, nonselective, and nonarbitrary, and to require judges to see to it that general laws are not applied sparsely, selectively, and spottily to unpopular groups" (p. 257). Also concurring, Justice Brennan argued, "When the punishment of death is inflicted in a trivial number of the cases in which it is legally available, the conclusion is virtually inescapable that it is being inflicted arbitrarily" (p. 294). He went on to write, "it smacks of little more than a lottery system" (p. 294).

Only two of the five concurring justices argued that the death penalty was in itself unconstitutional. This left the door open for states to rewrite their statutes in order to sway at least one of the other three justices to side with the dissenting opinion in future cases. One response to the *Furman* decision was the use of mandatory death penalty laws. These laws were intended to remove the arbitrariness of the imposition of death sentences. However, these laws were declared unconstitutional in ***Woodson v. North Carolina*** (1976). After *Woodson*, many state legislatures continued to reframe and reform their death penalty statutes.

Then, in ***Gregg v. Georgia*** (1976), the Court ruled that the death penalty was not a *per se* violation of the Eighth Amendment. The *Gregg* decision upheld a Georgia statute that required a number of new trial procedures intended to prevent the death penalty from being arbitrarily imposed. According to Latzer (2002), there were three major components in the Georgia statute. First, death sentences could only be imposed for homicides with aggravating factors and insufficient mitigating factors. Second, a bifurcated trial process was implemented where guilt and sentencing decisions were determined in separate proceedings. Once a defendant is found guilty, they would then move to a separate penalty proceeding where both aggravating and mitigating factors are presented prior to sentencing decisions. Last, the statue also provided a direct appeal in death penalty cases to the state's highest court. After the *Gregg* decision, the Georgia statue became the model for other states wishing to reinstate the death penalty.

Since the reinstatement of many death penalty statues after *Gregg*, there have been a number of noteworthy cases reviewed by the Supreme Court. In *McCleskey v. Kemp* (1987) the Court reviewed whether Georgia violated the Fourteenth Amendment's "equal protection" clause as well as the Eighth Amendment, based on arguments that the defendant's sentence was arbitrarily applied. The defendant, McClesky, was an African American man who was convicted and sentenced to death for a murder committed during a robbery. Using research evidence and a study conducted by David Baldus (known as the "**Baldus Study**"), the defendant suggested that the Georgia sentencing scheme discriminated based on the race of victims. The research presented suggested that offenders were more likely to receive the death penalty if their victim was white. The Court, however, rejected this defense and argued that defendants must prove that purposeful or intentional racial discrimination was used in their specific case. Thus, the Court ruled that the Baldus study was not sufficient evidence to declare the death penalty to be unconstitutional.

Additional Eighth Amendment challenges have taken place since McClesky; however, the use of the death penalty continued, and the number of executions grew until it peaked at 98 executions in 1999 (DPIC, 2011). Since then, the number of executions has drastically declined. In 2010, there were only 46 executions (DPIC, 2011). Some suggest that the drop in executions is due to states restricting their death penalty laws and adopting death penalty exemptions for offenders such as the mentally retarded and juveniles.

In Atkins v. Virginia (2002), the Supreme Court ruled that executing the mentally retarded was unconstitutional under the Eighth Amendment. Latzer (2002) explained that the Court "found a national consensus against executions of the retarded" (p. 255) after 17 death penalty states adopted statues against capital punishment for the mentally retarded. Then, in Roper v. Simmons (2005), the Court ruled that the death penalty for juveniles (offenders under the age of 18 at the time of offense) also violated the Eighth Amendment. The Court again looked at the evolving standards of decency and the extent to which states used and supported the death penalty for juvenile offenders. In both cases, the rulings suggest that our policies are moving toward a reduction in the use of the death penalty. Thus, even though the death penalty still exists in the United States, the extent of its use has significantly decreased and statutory limitations have been placed on its use.

Arbitrariness

One of the controversial issues surrounding capital punishment is whether it is arbitrarily applied. Many questions exist as to why some offenders receive a death sentence, while other offenders who committed a similar crime do not. Thus, the question as to whether like cases are treated alike is raised. As mentioned above, the Supreme Court justices argued in the *Furman* case that the death penalty must be fairly applied. In the *Furman* decision, the justices compared receiving the death penalty to being struck by lightning. The *Gregg* decision and the changes to death penalty statutes since then were intended to decrease issues of disparity and arbitrariness. However, a number of issues remain, and debates around the fairness in the application of death sentences continue.

Geography

One of the issues currently gaining attention is the geographic disparity in the use of capital punishment. Each year, criminal justice scholars meet at the annual meeting of the American Society of Criminology. In 2010, Robert Bohm, a leading death penalty scholar, discussed the geographic disparities in sentencing in his "Future of the Death Penalty" panel. Bohm discussed the fact that only a small portion of both states (and counties within states) account for a disproportionate number of death sentences. This suggests that an offender's chance of receiving the death penalty is highly predictable by the state (or county) in which the crime was committed.

According to the DPIC (2011), the majority of death sentences are carried out in the South and then the Midwest. Since 1976, there were 1,044 executions in the South (82%) and 149 executions in the Midwest (11.7%). The West only accounts for 5.8% (74) of executions and the Northeast has only executed 4 people (.3%). These numbers demonstrate that the death penalty is more commonly used in specific geographic portions of the United States.

Of the 34 states with the death penalty, a small minority of states account for the majority of executions. Baumgartner (2010) reviewed the 1,229 executions between 1976 and 2010 and found that just 10 of the death penalty states account for more than 80% of total executions. The top five states (Texas,

Virginia, Oklahoma, Florida, and Missouri) account for almost 65% of total executions. Moreover, just the top three states, Texas (463), Virginia (108), and Oklahoma (91), account for more than half (53.8%) of total executions in this country.

Baumgartner (2010) continues by examining the counties within the states that have sentenced offenders to death. He first suggests that only 454 U.S. counties (out of 3,146) have carried out an execution. In addition, the top five counties for executions (Harris County, Texas; Dallas County, Texas; Oklahoma County, Oklahoma; Tarrant County, Texas; and Bexar County, Texas) account for 21.16% of all executions nationwide. Harris County, Texas, alone has executed 115 offenders (9.36%). These numbers lend support for the argument that the death penalty is arbitrarily applied and that geographic disparities in the death penalty exist. It also demonstrates that only a minority of communities within the United States typically uses the death penalty as a form of punishment.

Race

The extent to which race of the offender or race of the victim impacts one's likelihood of receiving the death penalty is a subject of much debate and research among criminal justice scholars. Racial bias in sentencing has been a hotly contested issue during the post-slavery era, particularly in the South. Some scholars have suggested that state-sponsored executions served as a legal substitution for the lynching of blacks in the South during the late 1800s and early 1900s, while others suggest that legal executions actually increased the rate of lynchings during that time (Keil & Vito, 2009). A great deal of research has continued to be conducted in order to examine any racial biases in death sentences in more detail throughout the last 100 years.

Although the Supreme Court did not directly examine racial bias in the administration of the death penalty in *Furman*, del Carmen et al. (2005) suggest that racial discrimination was a salient issue in the case (even among two of the dissenting justices). They go on to state that Justice Douglas argued "the death sentence [was] disproportionately imposed and carried out on the poor, the Negro, and the members of the unpopular groups" (p. 46). The issue of racial discrimination was essentially attributed to the fact that death penalty was applied in an arbitrary and capricious manner.

As mentioned earlier, in the court case *McCleskey v. Kemp* (1987), the Supreme Court examined whether there was a violation of either the Eighth or Fourteenth Amendments due to racial disparities in sentencing. The results of the Baldus Study, presented during the McClesky case, indicated that "after controlling for the presence or absence of hundreds of variables for legitimate case characteristics, such as the level of violence and the defendant's prior record, defendants whose victims were white faced, on average, odds of receiving a death sentence that were 4.3 times higher than similarly situated defendants whose victims were black" (Baldus & Woodworth, 2003, p. 518). However, this study was not enough to declare the death penalty unconstitutional. Instead, defendants would have to prove that there was purposeful racial discrimination in each particular case. Although a violation of the Constitution was not found, the issue of racial disparities in sentences began to be researched further.

Then, in 1990, the General Accounting Office (GAO) published the results of a study that examined the empirical studies about racial disparities in death sentences that had been conducted since the *Furman* decision. Their findings were based on the evaluation of 28 published studies that met a minimal standard for research quality (with more than half of them rated as high or medium quality). They found that 82% of the studies found race of victim to be a significant predictor of receiving the death penalty. According to the studies, those who murder whites were more likely to receive the death penalty than those who murder blacks. In addition, the GAO report suggested that the influence of the race of victim was found at all stages of the criminal justice process. The analyses also showed "that after controlling statistically for legally relevant variables and other factors thought to influence death penalty sentencing (e.g., region, jurisdiction), differences remain in the likelihood of receiving the death penalty based on race of victim" (GAO, 1990, p. 6). Overall, the report suggests that the research has demonstrated a strong race of victim influence on death sentences.

The GAO Report (1990) also examined the relationship between race of defendant and the likelihood of receiving the death penalty, although this relationship was more complicated. For example, among the studies that found a significant relationship, more than 75% of them found that black defendants were more likely to receive the death penalty. However, the remaining studies found the relationship to be significant but in the other direction, with white defendants more likely to be sentenced to death than black defendants. The report suggested that:

> "The evidence for the influence of the race of defendant on the death penalty outcomes was equivocal. Although more than half of the studies found that race of defendant influenced the likelihood of being charged with a capital crime or receiving the death penalty, the relationship between race of defendant and outcome varied across studies. For example, sometimes the race of defendant interacted with another factor. In one study researchers found that in rural areas black defendants were more likely to receive death sentences, and in urban areas white defendants were more likely to

receive death sentences. In a few studies, analyses revealed that the black defendant/white victim combination was the most likely to receive the death penalty. However, the extent to which the findings was influenced by race of victim rather than race of defendant was unclear" (GAO, 1990, p. 6).

Baldus and Woodworth (2003) evaluated 18 additional studies that were published since the 1990 GAO report. They found similar results and continued support for the fact that offenders who murder white victims are more likely to receive the death penalty than offenders who murder black victims. Of the 18 studies Baldus and Woodworth examined, two found no race effect, three found both race of defendant and race of victim effects, two found effects in black defendant/white victim cases only, and 12 report race of victim effects but no race of defendant effects. Although the findings from these studies varied, they generally support the same conclusion of the 1990 GAO Report that a pattern of racial disparities exists.

Researchers continue to evaluate the relationship between race and the death penalty. Some suggest the racial disparities exist due partially to the prosecutorial discretion in the decision to seek the death penalty. According to del Carmen et al. (2005), "prosecutorial discretion plays a decisive role in how, when, and why capital murder charges are brought" (p. 50). As mentioned earlier, some prosecutors may choose to seek the death penalty for political reasons (Bohm, 2003). In addition, any bias among those making death penalty decisions may naturally translate into bias in the system. The DPIC (2011) notes that among death penalty states, 98% of district attorneys are white, while only 1% are black. With such a disproportionate number of black offenders sentenced to death it is not surprising that researchers are beginning to look at the racial identity of those who seek the death penalty.

Del Carmen et al. (2005) also discuss the relationship between racial bias and the legal community. Among prosecutors there may be bias in both the decision to seek a death sentence as well as during jury selection (i.e., excluding minority jurors). One practice they discuss is the use of "jury shuffling," where parties will move potential minority jurors to the back of the list so they are less likely to be selected. In addition, prosecutors are free to exercise their discretionary challenges during jury selection, and some may choose to remove minorities from the potential jury. Del Carmen et al. (2005) also suggest that information received from law enforcement may influence prosecutorial decisions. They report that "the amount of hard evidence may be different as police and sheriff's departments often pursue criminal activity in white neighborhoods more aggressively than crime in black or minority neighborhoods. Discrimination or racial bias on the part of law enforcement may have a significant and direct impact on prosecutor's ability to pursue the death penalty" (p. 51).

Class

Another issue in the death penalty debate is whether or not the death penalty is disproportionately imposed on the poor and indigent offenders. Much of this debate centers on inadequate representation and the use of court-appointed public defenders for indigent capital defendants. Del Carmen et al. (2005) suggest that "while some indigent capital defendants are given competent counsel, others are not," and they attribute this to the "social link between indigent capital offenders and court-appointed counsel" (p. 158). They go on to report that as many as 90% of capital defendants are indigent. According to the DPIC (2011), Justice Ruth Bader Ginsburg stated in 2001 that "people who are well represented at trial do not get the death penalty ... I have yet to see a death case among the dozens coming to the Supreme Court on eve-of-execution stay applications in which the defendant was well represented at trial" (p. 1).

Dieter (2011) discusses the fact that states vary greatly in the quality of representation that they both require and provide for indigent capital offenders. He suggests that differences exist in "the number of attorneys assigned, their experience in death penalty matters, their rate of pay, and the funding made available for defense investigators and experts" (p. 26). He goes on to suggest that these differences play a significant role in whether or not an offender will avoid a death sentence. Examples of public defenders who slept during trial, showed up drunk at court, or even those who failed to investigate critical facts in the case, have all added to the controversy surrounding capital offenders who cannot afford their own attorney.

Bohm (2007) briefly discusses discrimination based on social class by simply examining how the definition of murder has led to disparities in how we treat those who have caused harm to society. He notes that although hundreds of thousands of deaths each year are attributed to occupational diseases, preventable medical errors, tobacco-related diseases, unnecessary surgeries, and lethal industrial products, none of the people responsible for these deaths are sentenced to death. Only a small portion of these deaths are even considered intentional or criminally negligent. Bohm (2007) suggests that

> ... by virtue of their class position, the perpetrators of these "white-collar crimes," no matter how malicious and heinous their actions, simply are not considered appropriate candidates for capital punishment in the United States. Justice Douglas wrote in his Furman decision, "One searches our chronicles in vain for the execution

of any member of the affluent strata of this society." Former San Quentin warden Clinton T. Duffy stated that he knew of no one of means who was ever executed. Finally, as attorney Bryan Stevenson has pointed out, capital punishment really means "them without the capital gets the punishment." The reason wealth matters is that the wealthy are able to hire the best attorneys. In many capital cases, the outcome depends more on an attorney's skill than what actually happened (p. 306).

It is important to note, however, that the research available on the direct influence of class or social status on one's chances of receiving a death sentence is limited. Additional research, one that controls for the influence of all other potentially influential variables, still needs to be conducted.

Death Penalty Around the World

Much of the information about the use of the death penalty around the world comes from Amnesty International, a human rights organization. This organization opposes the use of the death penalty and has worked toward the abolition of the death penalty at the global level. Regardless of their stance on the death penalty, Amnesty International keeps some of the most up-to-date and centrally located information regarding the use of the death penalty in the world.

Amnesty International (2011) documents that there are 58 countries (see Table 1) classified as "retentionist," since they have retained the use of the death penalty. The United States is among those countries. However, Amnesty International argues that since 1977 (when their movement began), 123 countries have abolished the use of the death penalty. As of 2010, there are 139 total countries that have abolished the death penalty by law or in practice (i.e., it remains on the books but they don't use it). Overall, they report a trend toward abolition since more than 30 countries have abolished the death penalty in the past decade alone.

Amnesty International (2011) reports the top 10 countries that executed the most people in 2010. They are: (1) China; (2) Iran; (3) North Korea; (4) Yemen; (5) the USA; (6) Saudi Arabia; (7) Libya; (8) Syria; (9) Bangladesh; and (10) Somalia. China does not report official statistics on the number of executions, citing these as "state secrets"; however, the estimates are in the thousands. It is commonly believed that China executes more people each year than all other countries combined.

When it comes to the execution of juveniles, there are even fewer countries that execute offenders who were under the age of 18 at the time of the crime.

Table 1: Countries with the Death Penalty

Afghanistan	Guyana	Saint Kitts and Nevis
Antigua and Barbuda	India	Saint Lucia
Bahamas	Indonesia	Saint Vincent & the Grenadines
Bahrain	Iran	Saudi Arabia
Bangladesh	Iraq	Sierra Leone
Barbados	Jamaica	Singapore
Belarus	Japan	Somalia
Belize	Jordan	Sudan
Botswana	Kuwait	Syria
Chad	Lebanon	Taiwan
China	Lesotho	Thailand
Comoros	Libya	Trinidad and Tobago
Democratic Republic of Congo	Malaysia	Uganda
Cuba	Mongolia	United Arab Emirates
Dominica	Nigeria	United States of America
Egypt	North Korea	Vietnam
Equatorial Guinea	Oman	Yemen
Ethiopia	Pakistan	Zimbabwe
Guatemala	Palestinian Authority	
Guinea	Qatar	

*This table was compiled with information obtained from Amnesty International (2011).

Amnesty International (2011) reports that there have been 86 executions of juvenile offenders since 1990. It is important to note that this represents only a fraction of the number of executions worldwide. These executions were carried out by the following nine countries: China; Democratic Republic of Congo; Iran; Nigeria; Pakistan; Saudi Arabia; Sudan; the USA; and Yemen. One of the controversies surrounding the use of the death penalty for juveniles in the United States was due to the fact that this country is the only Western democracy on that list. One may argue that American society differs from the societies of many of those countries, yet we still used the same form of punishment, one that has been abandoned by most other democracies. It is reported "the USA and Iran have each executed more child offenders than the other eight countries combined and Iran has now exceeded the USA's total since 1990 of 19 child executions" (Amnesty International, 2011, p. 1).

Bohm (2007) suggested "the most flagrant U.S. deviation from the consensus of international law was its execution of juvenile offenders" (p. 140). He stated that the execution of juvenile offenders was "prohibited by the International Covenant on Civil and Political Rights, by the U.N. Convention on the Rights of the Child, and the American Convention on Human Rights" and goes on to suggest that "so broad is the acceptance of this prohibition that it is widely considered a norm of customary international law" (p. 140). As mentioned previously, the United States banned the execution of juvenile offenders in the Supreme Court case *Roper v. Simmons*

(2005). With this Supreme Court decision, the United States is now more in line with international standards pertaining to the execution of juveniles.

The continued use of the death penalty for adult offenders poses a number of political and international issues for the America. As more countries around the world abolish the use of the death penalty, many of these abolitionist countries look to the United States to do the same, since it is viewed as one of the international leaders on human rights. According to Bohm (2007), the death penalty is viewed as a human rights violation in Europe. All countries in the European Union have abolished the death penalty (as abolition is required for admittance). Bohm (2007) goes on to suggest that the European Union also considers a universal moratorium on executions and the death penalty's abolition as key factors in relations between the European Union and third countries. Member countries are to take this into account when finalizing agreements with third countries. Consequently, some foreign businesses, particularly those operated by governments, may make economic decisions based on a state's use of the death penalty (p. 139).

As we can see, the use of capital punishment in this country may directly affect international relations between the United States and our foreign allies.

> The position of the United States on the death penalty is contrary to the position of all other western-industrialized nations and all U.S. allies, except Japan. Retaining the death penalty may have significant political and economic repercussions. As Law Professor Richard Wilson observes, "[T]he United States risks bitter resentment and legitimate claims of hypocrisy by the community of nations if it continues to aggressively apply the death penalty while asserting a commitment to human rights at home and abroad" (Bohm, 2007, p. 142).

It is a commonly accepted belief that there is a growing international consensus against its use. However, the extent to which the continued use of the death penalty in the United States will influence foreign relationships in the future remains unknown.

Conclusion

Increased research in arbitrariness of the death penalty as well as foreign pressure for abolition makes the death penalty a "hot topic" of political debates. It is a topic that has garnered a great deal of public attention for decades. However, regardless of public support in the United States, research indicates that the use of the death penalty has continued to decrease since the late 1990s.

The extent to which the decrease in use is due to questions about arbitrariness, foreign pressures, the innocence debate, or a general decrease in public support for the penalty remains unknown.

Overall, it is important to note that removing all elements of bias and arbitrariness in the system is next to impossible. As mentioned previously in this chapter, capital punishment appears to be arbitrarily imposed based on characteristics such as the geographic area where a crime is committed, the race of offender and/or victim, as well as the socioeconomic class of the offender. Any system based on the actions and behaviors of human beings will find elements of bias and discrimination within the process. Many may even consider the complete elimination of arbitrariness in the administration of the death penalty is impossible. However, some may argue that due to the permanence and irreversibility of this sanction, we should abandon the use of the death penalty if the sanction cannot be consistently and fairly applied. Over the next few years, both supporters of the death penalty as well as abolitionists will continue to monitor the use of this sanction and will continue to research how it is imposed on offenders and victims.

References

Amnesty International. (2011, October 31). *Figures on the Death Penalty*. Retrieved from http://www.amnesty.org/en/death-penalty/numbers

Baldus, D. C., and Woodworth, G. (2003). Race discrimination and the death penalty: An empirical and legal overview. In Acker, J. R., Bohm, R. M., & Lanier, C. S. (eds.), *America's experiment with capital punishment: Reflections on the past, present, and future of the ultimate penal sanction* (pp. 27–54). Durham, NC: Carolina Academic Press.

Baumgartner, F. R. (2010). *The geography of the death penalty*. Retrieved from http://www.deathpenaltyinfo.org/documents/Baumgartner-geography-of-capital-punishment-oct-17-2010.pdf

Bohm, R. M. (2010, November). *The future of capital punishment in the United States*. Presented at the meeting of the American Society of Criminology, San Francisco, CA.

Bohm, R. M. (2003). American death penalty opinion: Past, present, and future. In Acker, J. R., Bohm, R. M., & Lanier, C. S. (eds.), *America's experiment with capital punishment: Reflections on the past, present, and future of the ultimate penal sanction* (pp. 27–54). Durham, NC: Carolina Academic Press.

Bohm, R. M. (2007). *Deathquest III: An introduction to the theory and practice of capital punishment in the United States*. Newark, NJ: Matthew Bender & Company, Inc.

del Carmen, R. V., Vollum, S., Cheeseman, K., Frantzen, D., and San Miguel, C. (2005). *The death penalty: Constitutional issues, commentaries, and case briefs*. Newark, NJ: Matthew Bender & Company, Inc.

Death Penalty Information Center (2011). *Facts about the death penalty* (Fact Sheet). Retrieved from http://www.deathpenaltyinfo.org

Dieter, R. C. (2011). *Struck by lightning: The continuing arbitrariness of the death penalty thirty-five years after its re-instatement in 1976.* Retrieved from Death Penalty Information Center website: http://www.deathpenaltyinfo.org

Keil, T. J., and Vito, G. F. (2009). Lynching and the death penalty in Kentucky, 1866–1934: Substitution or supplement? *Journal of Ethnicity in Criminal Justice, 7,* 53–68.

Latzer, B. (2002). *Death penalty cases: Leading U.S. Supreme Court cases on capital punishment.* Boston: Butterworth-Heinemann.

Severson, K. (2011, September 22). Georgia inmate executed; Raised racial issues in death penalty. *New York Times.* Retrieved from http://www.nytimes.com

U.S. General Accounting Office (1990). *Death penalty sentencing: Research indicates pattern of racial disparities.* Washington, DC: U.S. General Accounting Office.

Cited Cases

Atkins v. Virginia, 536 U.S. 304 (2002).
Furman v. Georgia, 408 U.S. 238 (1972).
Gregg v. Georgia, 429 U.S. 875 (1976).
McCleskey v. Kemp, 482 U.S. 920 (1987).
Roper v. Simmons, 543 U.S. 551 (2005).
Woodson v. North Carolina, 428 U.S. 280 (1976).

Learn More on the Internet

The Innocence Project:
   http://www.innocenceproject.org/
Frontline: Death by Fire:
   http://www.pbs.org/wgbh/pages/frontline/death-by-fire/

Discussion Questions

1. Should the United States continue to utilize the death penalty, or should the death penalty be abolished nationally?
2. In the United States, what improvements would need to be made to the death penalty to ensure that an innocent person is never executed?

SECTION 5

RACE, GENDER, THE EX OFFENDER, AND THE COMMUNITY

CHAPTER NINE

Inmate Reentry

By Richard Tewksbury and David Patrick Connor

Introduction

As a result of increasingly large numbers of incarcerated offenders in the United States, numerous individuals are returning to society from prison each year. There are currently over 1.6 million people living in American correctional facilities, and this translates into approximately 1 in every 199 people who are locked behind bars (Sabol & West, 2010). Because convicted felons, as a whole, are not generally sentenced to death or life without parole, it should not be surprising that the majority of these people—and nearly 650,000 of these individuals annually—are released from state and federal prisons (U.S. Department of Justice, 2011). Needless to say, corrections officials have always grappled with how to best approach the inevitable release of incarcerated offenders back into society. However, as more inmates complete their lengthy prison terms, the skyrocketing numbers of ex inmates returning to communities are catching the attention of citizens and policy makers, as well as criminal justice practitioners and scholars, promoting more serious discussions and examinations of prisoner reentry.

What Is Reentry?

Reentry can be defined as the process by which incarcerated offenders depart from correctional facilities and return to the outside community. This move from prison to free society often involves correctional programs and related community efforts aimed at facilitating successful reintegration among inmates. It may be argued that inmate reentry starts at the time of prison admission, and many criminologists contend that both correctional facilities and community correctional programs influence reintegration into society. Prison classification assignments, institutional programs, and appointments to community transition programs may center on reentry endeavors. As a result, **inmate reentry** is often considered to be the series of actions associated with the management of an individual's transition from incarceration to society (Travis, 2000). Emphasis is typically placed on the process and involves structures that move the transformation of imprisoned offenders to the status of a released ex inmate.

Although most inmates look forward to their release with great anticipation, those leaving correctional facilities are likely to encounter considerable stress on the outside. For many previously incarcerated individuals, the physical and mental pressures that come with returning to society prove to be very stressful and highly burdensome (Marston, 1993). The backwash of imprisonment may compromise the ability of newly released offenders to effectively resume their former roles in communities. Forced to construct new social identities for themselves, ex inmates subjected to the damaging effects of confinement may also struggle to rebuild and develop personal relationships that are critical to community connectedness. Prison inmates, largely removed from society, must effectively prepare to reenter an ever-changing world, in order to ready themselves for adjustment to life on the outside.

Interestingly, those coming back to society from prison are likely to encounter a broad range of reentry processes. This may explain, at least to a certain extent, the stressful nature of reentry. For instance, not all people in correctional facilities receive guidance about returning to the community prior to their release. As of the year before their anticipated out date, only about 1 in 10 inmates had participated in any type of formal reentry programs (Travis, 2005). Inmates, in some scenarios, prepare for their discharge from prison through security classification reductions. During these reclassification procedures, those approaching release are moved (or "brought down") from one security level to another, as well as transferred from one correctional facility to another. The final months of the custodial sentence, typically spent inside minimum-security facilities or prerelease centers, are often adorned with fewer institutional rules, fewer present staff members, and more personal liberty.

At the same time, a number of other offenders may participate in partial incarceration activities, such as work release and furlough programs. However, such opportunities are only available for a limited number of certain types of offenders, based on conviction type and length of sentence, and only in some jurisdictions. Sex offenders, for example, are ineligible to participate in these reentry endeavors. Inmates taking part in **work release** are permitted to leave correctional facilities for limited time periods to work at paid employment in the community, whereas prisoners allowed to go on **furlough** may be provided a temporary leave of absence from prison for family or educational purposes (Katz & Decker, 1982; Markley, 1973). Still, other incarcerated offenders may seek placement in a **halfway house**, which is a residence in the community that functions as a transitional environment between prison and society.

Many inmates, having already served a portion of their sentence, will rejoin society as parolees. Individuals released on **parole**—a conditional discharge from prison that occurs before the end of their maximum sentence—are afforded the opportunity to live on the outside under the control and legal custody of corrections authorities (Glaze & Bonczar, 2010). Other inmates will **serve out**, or complete, the entire duration of their sentence behind bars, returning to society without corrections officials overseeing their activities. Inmates who serve out their sentences return to society completely free and without any form of official supervision by criminal justice officials.

Because parole allows offenders to serve the last part of their prison sentence in the community, it may help ex inmates with their adjustment to outside life. For many parolees, such supervision will encourage good behavior and compliance that may prompt successful reintegration. When offenders serve their entire sentence in prison, they may not be exposed to the benefits of parole (Glaze & Bonczar, 2010). Parole conditions, for instance, often require offenders to attend community treatment programs. Additional conditions of release obligate ex inmates to refrain from crime and other conduct that is thought to be associated with the possibility of future criminal offenses. However, strict enforcement of these parole regulations may create unnecessary hardships for those released from prison. Adding to the stress inherent in reentry, many parolees must become effective time managers, simultaneously juggling meetings with parole officers, full-time employment, treatment program attendance, and all of the other aspects of leading a "regular" life. The parole officer, too, may serve as an essential confidante for released individuals seeking assistance and looking to avoid subsequent criminal behavior. And yet, **parole officers** are entrusted with the responsibility of providing both supervision and assistance to released offenders. These potentially incompatible roles leave parole officials with significant discretionary power that may interrupt parolee progress. The supervisory functions of parole officers may take precedence over their supportive role, particularly when caseloads are high and public pressure is strong to detect recidivism.

Despite the differences in release procedures and applicable supervision conditions, every inmate discharged from prison arguably experiences reentry. In other words, the process of reentering society impacts nearly every person sentenced to time behind bars (Petersilia, 2003). Because almost all inmates will one day leave prison, the majority of people housed in correctional facilities will undergo this distinctive transition period associated with rejoining society. For this reason, it is important to understand the demographics and other available information concerning released prison inmates.

Incarcerated individuals leaving prison are presently experiencing reentry in unprecedented numbers. In the year 2000, there were 604,858 inmates released from confinement in the United States, whereas by 2009 this number has risen to 729,295. From 2000 to 2009, the number of inmates released from state and federal correctional facilities increased by more than 20% (Sabol & West, 2010). However, the basic demographics of this expanding group of former inmates have not changed significantly over the past 10 years. While the number of people going through reentry has increased dramatically, the characteristics of this group has not changed.

The parole population continues to be largely male (88%), with white (41%) and African American (39%) offenders sharing dominance among released individuals. Further, more than one third (36%) of inmates released on parole have been incarcerated for a drug offense, and individuals convicted of violent (27%) and property (23%) offenses follow closely behind (Glaze & Bonczar, 2010). Although national demographics and corresponding crime information is not available for released individuals serving out their sentences, nearly 80% of released inmates are subjected to some form of community supervision (Austin, 2001). Thus, data on parolees largely reflects the entire prison population.

The majority of those returning to society from prison have serious medical and social problems, and many of these issues have not been properly addressed during the time of incarceration. Three-fourths of inmates leaving correctional facilities have a serious history of substance abuse (Hammett, Roberts, & Kennedy, 2001). Although many of these individuals have spent significant time behind bars, only 7 to 17% of those with confirmed alcohol and drug dependency issues receive treatment inside prison (National Institute on Drug Abuse, 2009). The pervasiveness of such addictions demonstrates that numerous individuals released from prison will need to participate in community substance abuse treatment programs, as chronic alcohol and drug use can lead to problems with maintaining employment.

Mental illness is also prevalent among prison inmates, as the incidence of serious mental illnesses is 2 to 4 times higher for incarcerated individuals than it is for the general population (Hammett et al., 2001). Many inmates suffer from schizophrenia, bipolar disease, major depression, posttraumatic stress disorder, and other serious mental illnesses. Unfortunately, conditions inside correctional facilities, coupled with insufficient prison mental health services, are often responsible for exacerbating rather than reducing or eliminating these problems. Left untreated and unstable in prison, people with serious mental illnesses returning to society may again break the law and return to correctional facilities.

In addition, chronic illnesses and communicable diseases are more widespread among those serving time in prison (National Commission on Correctional Health Care, 2002). For instance, in 1997, released inmates accounted for nearly one fourth of all people living with HIV or AIDS, almost one third of those determined to have hepatitis C, and more than one third of individuals diagnosed with tuberculosis (Hammett et al., 2001). More recently, in 2007, the most recent year for which general population data are available, the overall rate of estimated confirmed AIDS cases among state and federal inmates was 2.5 times greater than the general population rate (Maruschak & Beavers, 2009). Access to health care and related services for these individuals is fundamental to their successful reentry.

Former inmates rejoining society are limited in terms of educational achievements and employment experiences. Only 3 in every 5 inmates have obtained a high school diploma or its equivalent (Harlow, 2003). This limited education, coupled with low skill levels and extensive physical and mental health problems, almost guarantees employment difficulties that are common and accompanying low employment rates and earnings histories for people leaving prison. Unfortunately, these issues do not appear to be addressed adequately while inmates reside in prison. The percentage of the inmate population involved in vocational or educational programs is dropping in nearly all correctional systems and facilities (National Center on Addiction and Substance Abuse, 2010).

Housing difficulties, too, plague many people entering and exiting prison. In the months prior to their incarceration, more than 10% of individuals locked in prisons are homeless; further, released inmates who periodically resided in homeless shelters prior to their confinement were almost 5 times as likely to stay in such a location upon reentry (Metraux & Culhane, 2004). Although there are no national statistics on homelessness among people leaving prison, numbers from some major jurisdictions suggest a very grave situation nationwide. At any given time in Los Angeles and San Francisco, 30 to 50% of all parolees are without a home (Travis, Solomon, & Waul, 2001). In New York City, as many as 20% of released inmates are homeless or their housing arrangements are unstable (Supportive Housing Network of New York, 2002).

Barriers to Successful Reentry

Following release from incarceration, many ex inmates quickly discover considerable setbacks in the community. Despite their liberation from correctional facilities, former inmates may encounter various restrictions and limitations that make life on the outside more arduous (Petersilia, 2003).

Numerous barriers seemingly prevent formerly incarcerated individuals from effectively rejoining society. These obstacles to successful reentry encompass social stigma, housing difficulties, employment hardships, and civil disabilities. Such roadblocks inhibit the ability of many former offenders to become productive and law-abiding members of society.

Social Stigma

For many ex inmates, the stigma associated with imprisonment is perhaps the most obstructive barrier to successful reentry. In many cases, the **stigmatization**—setting a mark of disgrace upon a social group—that comes with a prison record is nearly insurmountable. There is considerable evidence that social stigma significantly hinders necessary aspects of societal reintegration, especially housing and employment opportunities for those previously incarcerated (Harding, 2003; Tewksbury, in press). Background checks and personal inquiries, for instance, have become customary for all applicants looking to rent an apartment or work in entry-level jobs. The stigma of incarceration and criminal conviction makes ex inmates unattractive candidates for even the most undesirable living spaces or jobs. As there are more people than jobs or available housing opportunities, it is not surprising that employers and landlords are likely to prefer the non-criminal to the individual just coming out of prison. Making matters worse, with a drop in the success of the American economy, finding employment may be especially difficult for newly released offenders, as the numbers of other (more desirable) candidates increases.

Beyond housing and employment predicaments, released inmates will likely experience difficult social encounters. Old friends and significant others, for example, may have nothing to do with the ex inmate, leaving him or her to fend for themselves, to be without important social supports. Or, conversely, such individuals may suddenly resurface in the lives of those previously incarcerated and introduce problems, challenges, and assorted other difficulties. Ex inmates must consequently learn how to manage the consequences of stigma for the purposes of developing a healthy social identity and place in the community. In doing so, many former inmates will likely endure substantial stress, which may cause them to backslide into criminal behavior (Harding, 2003). Released offenders are often labeled as potential hazards for personal relationships, and former acquaintances may intentionally distance themselves from ex inmates. Physical and emotional strain conceivably results from being stigmatized. If individuals continue to feel alienated because of their prison record, their chances at successful reentry become severely limited.

Housing Difficulties

The ability to acquire and maintain suitable housing is often the main concern for individuals returning to society from prison (Tewksbury & Connor, 2011). This is an immediate need, and it is one that the individual leaving prison knows must be addressed before the first night on the streets. However, for numerous ex inmates, securing a place to live may prove to be extremely challenging. Many released inmates do not have homes or families in which to return. This may be the result of lengthy incarcerations or strained family ties stemming from known criminal offenses. Parole conditions also potentially hamper housing opportunities for former inmates, as parolees are not allowed to associate with other convicted felons. Unfortunately, many people under parole supervision have family members or friends with felony convictions, and such parole stipulations preclude potential support from reformed acquaintances. Regardless, ex inmates with family and other social support should be considered highly fortunate, as these individuals are the minority among people exiting prison and reentering society.

For those released from incarceration without close social relationships, accessing suitable housing will likely be fraught with hardship. Because property owners often examine the credit history and criminal backgrounds of their prospective tenants, convicted felons are likely to be denied housing in the private market (Petersilia, 2003). Even if landlords refrain from such intrusive measures, most inmates returning to society do not have the necessary financial means to acquire their own personal residence. Similarly, ex inmates looking to find shelter through public housing may be easily disheartened. The **subsidized housing market**, which includes both public housing developments and housing generated through Section 8 vouchers, is unattainable (based on statutory law) for many convicted felons. Federal legislation dictates that subsidized housing providers may deny public housing services to individuals convicted of particular offenses, such as drug and sex crimes. When those released from prison are eligible for government accommodations, the limited availability of public housing often prevents individuals from receiving shelter for considerable periods of time, which may prove to be detrimental to the reintegration process.

For some convicted felons returning to society, the only real housing opportunity awaiting them may be a homeless shelter. Very much like public housing, however, accessibility remains problematic. Here, former offenders may encounter extensive waiting lists, as well as limited periods of time they are permitted to stay. Housing difficulties may also be especially acute for registered sex offenders, as residency restrictions in many jurisdictions prohibit such ex inmates from living near locations described as "child congregation" areas (Tewksbury & Connor, 2011). Such places are typically defined to include schools, parks, school playgrounds, daycare centers, bus stops, and recreational facilities. Fluctuating between 500 feet and 2,500 feet, residency restriction laws assert that specific distances must be preserved between a sex offender's residence and various landmarks in the community. Well over half of all states and numerous municipalities have sex offender residency restriction laws.

Employment Hardships

Employment opportunities for individuals released from prison have frequently been cited by scholars and experts as one of the most essential aspects for successful reintegration into society (Solomon, Johnson, Travis, & McBride, 2004; Travis, 2005). Released individuals with stable jobs can develop valuable skills and increase personal confidence, while simultaneously providing for themselves and their families (and therefore avoiding or minimizing many of the other challenges already discussed). At the same time, employment strengthens links to the outside community, and it reestablishes important structure and routine to the lives of former inmates, lessening the likelihood that offenders will revert to criminal activity. This proves to be vital, as many released offenders quickly move from the highly controlled environment of prison into the complex, unconstrained free world.

However, similar to housing difficulties, those returning to society from correctional facilities also face challenges related to employment (Fletcher, 2001; Pager, 2003). Many employers refuse to hire ex inmates, as individuals with criminal records may be perceived as unreliable, untrustworthy, or simply "bad for business." Business owners and hiring managers may be reluctant to accept responsibility for knowingly employing persons with criminal backgrounds, as liability issues surrounding ex inmate employees may place companies at risk of theft and workplace violence. Incarceration itself further compounds the matter, as time spent behind bars produces significant gaps in employment history, or perhaps even worse, creates an established record of menial labor assignments that calls attention to one's former status as "inmate." Unfortunately, those leaving prison are often bound for society without any marketable job skills.

Despite the fact that ex inmates may suffer employment difficulties as a direct result of their criminal records and incarcerations, legal barriers to employment are conceivably more discouraging. In many jurisdictions, individuals must obtain licenses in order to work in specific professions, such as teaching, nursing, and cosmetology. And yet, former offenders, particularly those convicted of felony offenses, are typically denied such legal authorization to work in these areas. For instance, in California, more than 260 occupations remain unavailable to former inmates (Samuels & Mukamal, 2004). Because of these obstacles to employment, individuals who have served time behind bars must deal with the likely possibility that their prospective lifetime earnings will be significantly decreased. Formerly incarcerated individuals may experience a 10% decrease in earnings over their lifetimes (Western & Pettit, 2000). These limitations, together with likely encountered failed attempts and discouragements from employers, may compel ex inmates to accept low-paying jobs that require little skill, because nothing better is available. In such situations, it is easy to see how such a situation could conceivably prompt their return to criminal activity.

Civil Disabilities

In accordance with federal law and the laws of many states, convicted felons endure associated repercussions that persist long after their prison sentences have been served and community supervision obligations have been met (Petersilia, 2003). Indeed, many ex inmates must reckon with the loss of their civil rights. These released individuals are no longer considered full citizens, and many encounter **civil disabilities**—the loss of certain legal rights resulting from criminal conviction—that preclude them from retaining the essential rights afforded to other members of society. These statutory restrictions function as additional, and often relentless and permanent, punishments for those attempting to move on with their lives.

The rights to vote and to hold public office are among the myriad legal restrictions that disqualify convicted felons from full civil and societal participation. Strikingly, in five states that block ex inmates from voting, as many as one fourth of African American men are permanently inhibited from engaging in the democratic process (King, 2008). Convicted felons may never again be legally permitted to own or possess firearms. Individuals discharged from correctional facilities may also find themselves stripped of their jury and parental privileges. Further, prohibitions on occupational licensing mentioned earlier are derived from these civil ineligibility laws. Although many jurisdictions allow for a process by which the state may restore a select number of civil rights after some period, some states permanently restrict certain rights for convicted felons.

Recidivism Rates

For many previously incarcerated individuals, the experience of confinement proves to be an extremely onerous experience. Those behind bars are often separated from their families, friends, and larger society for extensive periods of time. For this reason, it may seem rather implausible that a significant portion of former offenders would return so swiftly to the undesirable world of prison.

And yet, the numerous barriers facing inmates leaving prison discussed above clearly make meaningful progress exceedingly difficult in society (Petersilia, 2003). Because successful adjustment to life on the outside is riddled with these daunting obstacles, many ex inmates are unable to effectively reenter society without resuming criminal activity. Many of these recidivists subsequently find themselves back in correctional facilities.

Recidivism among ex inmates is commonly referred to as the repeated or habitual relapse into criminal behavior. It is considered the act of reoffending or participating in crime again, despite earlier police detections, court convictions, and possible correctional punishments. A recent study examining recidivism in 41 states found that more than 4 in 10 individuals released from prison returned to state correctional facilities within three years of their release (Pew Center on the States, 2011). Thus, it can be said that about half of all former inmates go back to prison within 3 years of their initial release back into society. Many other studies concerning criminal recidivism have revealed large proportions of persons released from prison who were eventually rearrested, reconvicted, or returned to prison within a specific time period. For instance, one national study found that, within three years of their discharge, 67.5% of released inmates were rearrested for a new offense, 46.9% were reconvicted for a new offense, and 25.4% were resentenced to prison for a new offense. Collectively, 51.8% of these previously incarcerated individuals were returned to correctional facilities, ordered to serve prison time for new convictions or technical parole violations (Langan & Levin, 2002). As a result, the overwhelming conclusion has been that the inmate population largely consists of habitual criminals, and correctional facilities that house these offenders do little to modify their criminal and deviant behavior.

Formerly incarcerated individuals are returned to prison for two reasons. The most obvious reason is continued criminal activity that results in a new criminal conviction. Perhaps a woman previously convicted of arson has once more pled guilty to intentionally setting her own home on fire, or maybe a convicted drug dealer has now been found guilty at trial of assaulting a police officer. Among individuals removed from parole supervision in 2009, approximately 9% of ex inmates returned to prison as a result of a new criminal conviction (Glaze & Bonczar, 2010). For those released on parole, **technical violations** of community supervision conditions may also send them back to prison. Perhaps a man convicted of manufacturing methamphetamine fails to report to his parole officer, or maybe a convicted sex offender fails to complete the required treatment program. Among individuals found guilty of violating parole in 2009, approximately 24% of ex inmates returned to prison for technical violations (Glaze & Bonczar, 2010).

Higher rates of recidivism and return to prison exist among parolees than for those released without supervision. This is likely due to the close monitoring of parolees and restrictive conditions of parole supervision. When under parole (or other) supervision, it is more likely that an authority figure can and will find something illegal or simply wrong in the behavior of an individual. In 2009, released individuals found in violation of their parole conditions accounted for 33.1% of all prison admissions, 35.2% of state prison admissions, and 8.2% of admissions to federal prisons (Sabol & West, 2010).

Recent Legal Developments in Reentry

In recent years, federal legislation has resulted in the funding of programs that have inspired innovation and some progress among inmate reentry policies and procedures. In April 2008, the **Second Chance Act** (P.L. 110-199) was signed into law. This legislation aims to exclusively enhance outcomes for individuals returning to society from prison. This act, administered by the Bureau of Justice Assistance, U.S. Department of Justice, authorizes federal grants to government entities and nonprofit organizations to improve inmate reentry efforts by providing services that can potentially help reduce recidivism. Second Chance grant programs include important aspects of the reentry process, particularly housing assistance, employment programs, and treatment curricula. The program received $25 million in 2009, with a total of 68 reentry grants awarded. In 2010, it received $100 million, and 188 grants were assigned (Clement, Schwarzfeld, & Thompson, 2011).

In 2004, the **Mentally Ill Offender Treatment and Crime Reduction Act** (MIOTCRA) was enacted by the federal government. Under this act, the Justice and Mental Health Collaboration Program (JMHCP) was established to assist states and local jurisdictions in bringing about cooperative efforts between criminal justice officials and mental health professionals. In this way, the legislation attempts to focus on people with mental illnesses, including ex inmates, to increase public safety and improve community treatment. Congress, in 2008, extended the MIOTCRA program for an additional 5 years. The program received $10 million in 2009, with a total of 43 grants awarded. In 2010, it received $12 million, and 62 grants were awarded (Clement et al., 2011).

The Residential Substance Abuse Treatment (RSAT) for State Prisoners Program was established by the **Violent Crime Control and Law Enforcement Act of 1994** (P.L. 103-322). RSAT helps state and local governments with the development of substance abuse treatment programs in correctional facilities and the community. The program received just under $10 million in 2009, and it increased to $28 million in 2010 (Clement et al., 2011). However, it is important to note that this legislation, as well as the Second Chance Act grant programs and JMHCP grants, depend on Congressional funding. With the current economic climate and major government cutbacks in funding for social programs, financial resources backing inmate reentry are likely to be reduced.

State legislation has also seemingly prioritized inmate reentry efforts in recent years. Virginia, for example, has enacted several laws concerning the reintegration of its prison population (Virginia Department of Corrections, 2010). Upon taking office in January 2010, Governor Robert McDonnell appointed the state's first prisoner reentry coordinator, and he created an advisory council to examine ways in which state, private, and faith-based groups may better plan for an individual's return to society. In 2011, McDonnell and his staff pushed several bills to help inmates get adjusted to society. Virginia lawmakers passed a law (SB 923), which became effective January 2012, requiring the Department of Corrections to establish a personal trust account for each inmate. Monetary funds received by inmates will have 10% removed by corrections officials and deposited into personal trust accounts designated for their release. Funds held in personal trust accounts will be paid to inmates upon their release. Other recent reentry initiatives in Virginia authorize certain inmates to temporarily leave correctional facilities to perform maintenance on state cemeteries and rest stops.

Aiming to decrease conditional release revocation rates by 20%, Kansas legislators in 2008 developed a Risk Reduction Initiative (SB 14) that awards funding to community corrections agencies to improve risk reduction efforts among offenders (Kansas Department of Corrections, 2008). The law also affords inmates a 60-day time credit for completing educational, vocational, and treatment programs to reduce their prison sentences. In 2007, Arizona lawmakers established a Teaching Offenders to Live Program (TOLP), which prepares incarcerated individuals for independent living in the community through treatment and relapse prevention training (Arizona Department of Corrections, 2011). The law (HB 2298) also requires many parole violators to participate in TOLP prior to their revocation hearing. If these individuals successfully complete the program, the Department of Corrections may advocate on behalf of such offenders, recommending parole reinstatement rather than incarceration.

Contemporary Reentry Programs

Despite the fact that previously incarcerated individuals face tremendous obstacles on the outside, programs aimed at assisting ex inmates are not necessarily commonplace. However, the following contemporary reentry programs highlight promising efforts that may provide valuable guidance to those newly released into society. Based in Kentucky, **Prodigal Ministries** is a Christian aftercare program that helps men and women avoid returning to prison (Council of State Governments Justice Center, 2011). The program starts working with offenders six months prior to their release. Although potential participants must apply and undergo an interview process, Prodigal Ministries offers many services for those accepted into the program. In particular, ex inmates are provided with residential housing and programs on an individual basis through case management, with a focus on recovery from substance abuse addictions.

Focused in Los Angeles, California, **New Start LA** provides transitional employment and job placement services to 100 ex inmates at a time exiting the California prison system (Council of State Governments Justice Center, 2011). Potential participants must be referred by their parole officer. The New Start program utilizes community partnerships in order to assist formerly incarcerated individuals. The Chicago School of Psychology provides both individual and group counseling for participating ex inmates, and Friends Outside Los Angeles County developed a job training program in cooperation with the One-Stop Employment Centers with a specific focus on the special needs of former inmates. Also, representatives from One-Stop in South Los Angeles meet regularly with case managers to discuss the progress of participants. For those ex inmates identified as lacking job skills, the One-Stop Employment Centers will provide paid transitional employment or job training to enhance employment outcomes. All One-Stop and partner staff complete a training certification program focused on formerly incarcerated individuals to improve services to ex inmate participants.

Offenders About to Reenter Society (OARS) is a reintegration program for Florida Department of Corrections inmates returning to Duval County (Jacksonville), Florida (Council of State Governments Justice Center, 2011). The program contains both pre- and post-release components and services. Prior to their release, inmates in OARS participate in cognitive behavioral programming, job skills training, parenting classes, and victim awareness sessions. Case management and planning, including input from both pre- and post-release staff, is also an essential component of this program. Following their release from prison, ex inmates are transported to the Jacksonville Reentry Center (JREC). Here, job skills training and character development classes are provided. Assistance with housing, substance abuse, and transportation is also available.

These are just a handful of the many programs that are available around the country designed to provide to reentering inmates support, assistance, and direction in establishing a crime-free, conventional, and healthy life. However, many of these programs are small (at most, serving a few dozen offenders at a time) and largely or wholly dependent on funding that is unstable, temporary, and almost always insufficient to allow full realization of program goals and objectives. In such cases, while some offenders reentering society may benefit, there remain many more who are left to contend with the challenges and barriers to successful reentry on their own.

Conclusion

Numerous individuals are approaching release from prison each year, and this is likely the result of increasingly large numbers of offenders being sentenced to prison. As more inmates complete their lengthy prison terms, the skyrocketing numbers of ex inmates returning to communities are encouraging more serious discussions and examinations of inmate reentry. Reentry is simply the process by which incarcerated offenders depart from correctional facilities and return to the outside community.

Although most inmates look forward to their release with great anticipation, exiting prison can be a shocking experience. For many previously incarcerated individuals, the physical and mental pressures associated with returning to society can have an overwhelmingly emotional impact. Newly released individuals often have serious medical and social problems, and many of these issues are not being properly addressed during their incarceration. Former inmates rejoining society are also frequently limited in terms of educational pursuits and employment experiences. To make matters worse, many barriers exist that prevent formerly incarcerated individuals from effectively rejoining society. Social stigma, housing difficulties, employment hardships, and civil disabilities inhibit the ability of many former offenders to become productive and law-abiding members of society. Many of these ex inmates subsequently find themselves back in correctional facilities as recidivists. Recidivism is commonly referred to as the repeated or habitual relapse into criminal behavior.

In recent years, federal and state legislation has apparently prioritized and inspired inmate reentry efforts. Despite these legislative endeavors, programs aimed at assisting ex inmates are not necessarily commonplace. However, several contemporary reentry programs highlight promising efforts that may provide valuable guidance to those newly released into society. To ensure that ex inmates do not involve themselves in future criminal activity, it is critical that such programs flourish, and correctional facilities and community programs must offer programming and preparation designed to facilitate successful reentry.

References

Arizona Department of Corrections. (2011). *Arizona Department of Corrections data and information*. Phoenix, AZ: Author. Retrieved September 4, 2011, from http://www.azcorrections.gov/data_info_081111.pdf

Austin, J. (2001). Prisoner reentry: Current trends, practices, and issues. *Crime & Delinquency, 47*(3), 314–334.

Clement, M., Schwarzfeld, M., & Thompson, M. (2011). *The National Summit on Justice Reinvestment and Public Safety: Addressing recidivism, crime, and corrections spending.* New York: Council of State Governments Justice Center.

Council of State Governments Justice Center. (2011). *Reentry programs database.* Retrieved September 4, 2011, from http://reentrypolicy.org/reentry-program-examples/reentry-programs-start

Fletcher, D. (2001). Ex-offenders, the labor market and the new public administration. *Public Administration, 79*(4), 871–891.

Glaze, L. E., & Bonczar, T. P. (2010). *Probation and parole in the United States, 2009.* (Bureau of Justice Statistics Publication No. NCJ 231674). Washington, DC: U.S. Department of Justice, Bureau of Justice Statistics. Retrieved September 4, 2011, from http://bjs.ojp.usdoj.gov/content/pub/pdf/ppus09.pdf

Harding, D. (2003). Jean Valjean's dilemma: The management of ex-convict identity in the search for employment. *Deviant Behavior, 24*(6), 571–595.

Hammett, T., Roberts, C., & Kennedy, S. (2001). Health-related issues in prisoner reentry. *Crime& Delinquency, 47*(3), 390–409.

Harlow, C. W. (2003). *Education and correctional populations.* (Bureau of Justice Statistics Publication No. NCJ 195670). Washington, DC: U.S. Department of Justice, Bureau of Justice Statistics. Retrieved September 4, 2011, from http://bjs.ojp.usdoj.gov/content/pub/pdf/ecp.pdf

Kansas Department of Corrections. (2008). *House Substitute for Senate Bill 14: Annual report.* Topeka, KS: Author. Retrieved September 4, 2011, from http://www.doc.ks.gov/publications/the-senate-bill-14-risk-reduction-initiative/SB_14_Risk_Reduction_Initiative_Report_2008.pdf

Katz, J. F., & Decker, S. H. (1982). An analysis of work release: The institutionalization of unsubstantiated reforms. *Criminal Justice and Behavior, 9*(2), 229–250.

King, R. S. (2008). *Expanding the vote: State felony disenfranchisement reform, 1997–2008.* Washington, DC: Sentencing Project.

Langan, P. A., & Levin, D. J. (2002). *Recidivism of prisoners released in 1994.* (Bureau of Justice Statistics Publication No. NCJ 193427). Washington, DC: U.S. Department of Justice,Bureau of Justice Statistics. Retrieved September 4, 2011, from http://bjs.ojp.usdoj.gov/content/pub/pdf/rpr94.pdf

Markley, C. W. (1973). Furlough programs and conjugal visiting in adult correctional institutions. *Federal Probation, 37*(1), 19–26.

Marston, J. L. (1993). Stress and stressors: Inmate and staff perceptions. *American Jails, 7*(4), 21–30.

Maruschak, L. M., & Beavers, R. (2009). *HIV in prisons, 20072008.* (Bureau of Justice Statistics Publication No. NCJ 228307). Washington, DC: U.S. Department of Justice, Bureau of Justice Statistics. Retrieved September 4, 2011, from http://bjs.ojp.usdoj.gov/content/pub/pdf/hivp08.pdf

Metraux, S. & Culhane, D. P. (2004). Homeless shelter use and reincarceration following prison release: Assessing the risk. *Criminology & Public Policy, 3*(2), 201–222.

National Center on Addiction and Substance Abuse. (2010). *Behind bars II: Substance abuse and America's prison population.* New York: Author. Retrieved September 4, 2011, from http://www.casacolumbia.org/articlefiles/575-report2010behindbars2.pdf

National Commission on Correctional Health Care. (2002). *The status of soon-to-be-released prisoners: A report to Congress.* Chicago: Author. Retrieved September 4, 2011, from http://www.ncchc.org/pubs/pubs_stbr.html

National Institute on Drug Abuse. (2009). *Treating offenders with drug problems: Integrating public health and public safety.* Bethesda, MD: Author. Retrieved September 4, 2011, from http://www.drugabuse.gov/pdf/tib/drugs_crime.pdf

Pager, D. (2003). The mark of a criminal record. *American Journal of Sociology, 108*(5), 937 975.

Petersilia, J. (2003). *When prisoners come home: Parole and prisoner reentry.* New York: Oxford University Press.

Pew Center on the States. (2011). *State of recidivism: The revolving door of America's prisons.* Washington, DC: The Pew Charitable Trusts. Retrieved September 4, 2011, from http://www.pewcenteronthestates.org/uploadedFiles/Pew_State_of_Recidivism.pdf

Sabol, W., & West, H. C. (2010). *Prisoners in 2009.* (Bureau of Justice Statistics Publication No. NCJ 231675). Washington, DC: U.S. Department of Justice, Bureau of Justice Statistics. Retrieved September 4, 2011, from http://bjs.ojp.usdoj.gov/content/pub/pdf/p09.pdf

Samuels, P., & Mukamal, D. (2004). *After prison: Roadblocks to reentry. A report on state legal barriers facing people with criminal records.* New York: Legal Action Center.

Solomon, A. L., Johnson, K. D., Travis, J., & McBride, E. C. (2004). *From prison to work: The employment dimensions of prisoner reentry.* Washington, DC: Urban Institute Press.

Supportive Housing Network of New York. (2002). *Blueprint to end homelessness in New York City.* New York: Author.

Tewksbury, R. (in press). *Stigmatization of sex offenders.* Tewksbury, R., & Connor, D. P. (2011). Needs of sex offenders approaching release: Report prepared for the Kentucky State Reformatory.

Travis, J. (2000). *But they all come back: Rethinking prisoner reentry.* (National Institute of Justice Publication No. NCJ 181413). Washington, DC: U.S. Department of Justice, Office of Justice Programs, National Institute of Justice.

Travis, J. (2005). *But they all come back: Facing the challenges of prisoner reentry.* Washington, DC: Urban Institute Press.

Travis, J. (2005). Prisoner reentry: The iron law of imprisonment. In R. Muraskin (ed.), *Key Correctional Issues* (pp. 65–66). Upper Saddle River, NJ: Prentice Hall.

Travis, J., Solomon, A. L., & Waul, M. (2001). *From prison to home: The dimensions and consequences of prisoner reentry.* Washington, DC: Urban Institute Press.

U.S. Department of Justice (2011). *Reentry.* Retrieved September 4, 2011, from http://www.ojp.usdoj.gov/reentry

Virginia Department of Corrections. (2010). *Virginia Adult Re-entry Initiative: The four year strategic plan.* Richmond, VA: Author. Retrieved September 4, 2011, from http://www.vadoc.state.va.us/documents/reentryInitiativeExecSummary.pdf

Western, B., & Pettit, B. (2000). Incarceration and racial inequality in men's employment. *Industrial and Labor Relations Review, 54*(1), 3–16.

Learn More on the Internet

Research from the Urban Institute on Reentry:
   http://www.urban.org/justice/corrections.cfm
Second Chance Act:
   http://reentrypolicy.org/government_affairs/second_chance_act

Discussion Questions

1. Many inmates will rejoin society as parolees. What are the advantages and disadvantages of parole supervision? For corrections officials? For offenders? For society?

2. Numerous barriers seemingly prevent formerly incarcerated individuals from effectively rejoining society. Which of these identified obstacles to successful reentry is likely to be the most difficult for ex offenders to overcome? Why?

CHAPTER TEN

Disenfranchisement

By Cherie Dawson Edwards

Introduction

Felon disenfranchisement refers to the practice of temporarily or permanently barring convicted felons from voting. The manner in which a convicted felon is disenfranchised varies by state. Currently, 48 states disenfranchise prisoners; 30 states disenfranchise probationers, and 35 states disenfranchise parolees (The Sentencing Project, 2011). Convicted felons remain the only directly disenfranchised population across the nation upheld by constitutional law (Johnson-Parris, 2003). Historically, the felon's separation from the democratic process dates beyond the beginning of American society (Special Project, 1970; Thompson, 2002); however, the contemporary application of felon disenfranchisement laws are embedded in the post–Civil War period when the American electorate demographically shifted due to the passage of the Reconstruction Amendments (13th, 14th, and 15th) passed in the 1800s.

Felon voting prohibitions did not originally account for the number of offenses that would become modern-day felonies or the subsequent drastic increases in the U.S. correctional population. The Unites States incarceration boom of the 1990s can be attributed to Drug War legislation that created offenses such as intent to distribute and conspiracy to distribute a controlled substance (see Dawson-Edwards, C., 2011). Mauer (2011a) reported that African Americans made up 80% of those charged for crack cocaine offenses, illustrating how the War on Drugs has had a tremendous impact on the color of incarceration in the United States.

As of year-end 2008, the U.S. prison population had reached 2.4 million (see Sabol, West, & Cooper, 2010) with 900,000 African Americans now incarcerated (Mauer, 2011a). The rates of incarceration for people of color collaterally impact the political engagement of African Americans (Dawson-Edwards, 2011). According to Manza and Uggen (2006), almost two million African Americans are barred from voting due to felony disenfranchisement.

This increase appears to have broad detrimental consequences for African American men. A reported 13% of African American men in the United States are unable to vote because of felony convictions (Fellner & Mauer, 1998).

The History of Felon Disenfranchisement

Early U.S. criminal disenfranchisement laws prohibited all criminals from voting. For example, Alabama's 1819 state constitution read: "Laws shall be made to exclude from ... suffrage, those who shall thereafter be convicted of bribery, perjury, forgery, or other high crimes or misdemeanors." However, in 1901, the new Alabama state constitution was revised to include:

> *All idiots and insane persons; those who shall by reason of conviction of crime be disqualified from voting at the time of the ratification of this Constitution; **those who shall be convicted of treason, murder, arson, embezzlement, malfeasance in office, larceny, receiving stolen property, obtaining property or money under false pretenses, perjury, subornation of perjury, robbery, assault with intent to rob, burglary, forgery, bribery, assault and battery on the wife, bigamy, living in adultery, sodomy, incest, rape, miscegenation, crime against nature, or any crime punishable by imprisonment in the penitentiary, or of any infamous crime or crime involving moral turpitude;** also, any person who shall be convicted as a vagrant or tramp, or of selling or offering to sell his vote or the vote of another, or of buying or offering to buy the vote of another, or of making or offering to make a false return in any election by the people or in any primary election to procure the nomination or election of any person to any office, or of suborning any witness or registrar to secure the registration of any person as an elector (A.L. Const. § 182, 1901).*

Modifications to criminal disenfranchisement laws strategically occurred as the country shifted from an era of slavery to the post–Civil War Reconstruction period. Prior to the Civil War, African slaves were counted as three fifths of a person for the purpose of apportionment, or allocating representatives and electors based on "numbers," which included "all other persons" or slaves (Chin, 2004). With the passage of the Thirteenth Amendment in 1965, slaves became whole persons and drastically increased the Southern populace. As a result, four million former slaves now fell into the class of "free persons" who were not entitled to political rights. According to Du Bois (1935, 1962, 1995), Congressman Stephens stated:

This emancipated multitude has no political status. Emancipation vitalizes only natural rights, not political rights. Enfranchisement alone carries with it political rights, and these emancipated millions are no more enfranchised now than when they were slaves. They never had political power. Their masters had a fraction of power as masters (p. 289).

This increase in a population of "free persons" with no political status shifted the representation of Southern states in the U.S. Congress, giving them tremendous political power until 1870 when the Fifteenth Amendment was ratified (Chin, 2004). Twenty years of seeing the impact of enfranchising former slaves, Southern states began to craft or revise criminal disenfranchisement laws to strategically include criminal offenses that were more likely to be committed by emancipated slaves. South Carolina reportedly included crimes that African Americans were more likely to commit such as: "thievery, adultery, arson, wife-beating, housebreaking, and attempted rape" (Fellner & Mauer, 1998, p. 3). Crimes that Whites were just as likely to commit, such crimes as murder or fighting, were not included on the disenfranchising crimes list (Shapiro, 1993; Fellner & Mauer, 1998).

Proceedings from the disenfranchising conventions of Mississippi (1890), South Carolina (1895), Alabama (1901), and Virginia (1901–1902) all demonstrate voter suppression as their purpose for creative disenfranchising laws that targeted African Americans (Rose, 1906; Shapiro, 1993; Dawson-Edwards, 2011). At the 1906 Virginia Convention, Delegate William A. Dunning stated "Everybody knows that this Convention has done its best to disfranchise the Negro" (Hench, 1998, p. 739). Virginia Delegate Carter Glass was recorded as saying that felon disenfranchisement was designed to eliminate "every Negro voter who can be gotten rid of" (Hench, 1998). In the 1965 court case *U. S. v. Mississippi*, the U.S. Supreme Court found that the convention held in 1890 "worked so well in keeping the Negro from voting … that by 1899 the percentage of qualified voters in the State who were Negros had declined from over 50% to about 9%, and by 1954 only about 5% of the Negros of voting age in Mississippi were registered" (Hench, 1998, p. 741).

> "Everybody knows that this Convention has done its best to disfranchise the Negro"
>
> —Virginia Convention, Delegate William A. Dunning (1906)

The right of citizens of the United States to vote shall not be denied or abridged by the United States or by any State on account of race, color, or previous condition of servitude (U.S. Const. Amend. XV, 1).

Male freed slaves were enfranchised in 1870 when the Fifteenth Amendment was ratified. Since that time, there have been numerous direct and indirect attempts at disenfranchising minority voters. State felon voting prohibitions are the sole remaining technique of disenfranchisement. All others have been outlawed. The U.S. Supreme Court has long acknowledged that felon disenfranchisement is a discriminatory voting restriction allowed by Section 2 of the Fourteenth Amendment (*Green v. Board of Elections*, 1967; Johnson-Parris, 2003). The ruling was based on the "other crime" exception explicitly stated in Section 2:

*When the right to vote at any election … is denied to any of the male inhabitants of such State, being twenty-one years of age, and citizens of the United States, or in any way abridged, **except for participation in rebellion, or other crime**, the basis of representation therein shall be reduced in the proportion which the number of such male citizens shall bear the whole number of male citizens twenty-one years of age in such State* (U.S. Const. Amend. XIV, 2).

Historians have argued and politicians have admitted that the race-neutral language of Section 2 was purposeful and utilized at the time because it was "politically inadvisable to go to the country … on a platform having anything to do with Negro suffrage" (Bickel, 1955; Chin, 2004, p. 267). Section 2 did not grant voting rights for the newly emancipated former slaves; however, it did encourage states to grant the franchise to freed slaves or face the penalty of losing seats in Congress (Chin, 2004). The exploitation of the **"other crime exception"** was the only way to simultaneously suppress the African American vote and avoid a reduction in congressional representation. While the Fourteenth Amendment only encouraged, the Fifteenth Amendment guaranteed the African American vote.

The relationship between felon disenfranchisement laws and the Fourteenth Amendment was further clarified In *Richardson v. Ramirez* (1974) (Behrens, 2004; Johnson-Parris, 2003; Price, 2002). In *Richardson*, the Equal Protection Clause of the Fourteenth Amendment was used to argue the unconstitutionality of California's ex felon voting restriction

(Behrens, 2004). More specifically, the claim suggested that an ex offender's full reintegration into society is inhibited by the inability to vote. Additionally, they argued that the law discriminated against them on account of race. The Court ruled the California felon disenfranchisement law did not violate the U.S. Constitution, and ruled that states are constitutionally authorized to disenfranchise convicted felons (Behrens, 2004).

The Fourteenth Amendment and Felon Disenfranchisement

Since the penning of the Fourteenth Amendment, the U.S. Supreme Court has developed three levels of scrutiny to determine equal protection violations: rational basis, heightened scrutiny, and strict scrutiny. **Rational basis**, the lowest level of review, requires the law to have a rational association to a legitimate governmental purpose (Price, 2002). The middle level, **heightened scrutiny**, requires a "fair and substantial" relationship between the means and legitimate governmental interest (Samaha, 2003). Heightened scrutiny is usually reserved for gender classifications. The final standard, strict scrutiny, is usually applied to racial classifications and provides that the government must show that the law is essential to furthering a "compelling governmental interest" (Samaha, 2003; Price, 2002). However, the U.S. Supreme Court has declared voting as a fundamental right, making any restrictions on that right subject to a strict scrutiny analysis under the Equal Protection Clause (Chin, 2004).

Many voting restrictions have failed to survive strict scrutiny. The homeless (*Collier v. Menzel*, 1985), mentally incompetent persons (*Doe v. Rowe*, 2001), pretrial detainees (*Murphree v. Winter*, 1984) and individuals receiving governmental assistance (*U.S. v. Andrews*, 1972), have all had statutory voting prohibitions, only to be granted their rights through case law based on equal protection (Chin, 2002). In fact, prior to the *Richardson* decision, Section 1—the Equal Protection Clause—was successfully used in several lower-level courts to invalidate felon voting prohibitions (Chin, 2002). For example, in *Stephens v. Yeomans* (1970) the U.S. District Court for the District of New Jersey found New Jersey's felon voting prohibition to be in violation of the Fourteenth Amendment's Equal Protection Clause. They held that the "irrational and inconsistent" classifications were unconstitutional because they did not possess "exacting standards of precision required by the equal protection clause" when applied to voting restrictions (*Stephens v. Yeomans*, 1970, p. 1188; Thompson, 2002).

There have been other successful applications of the equal protection argument as it related to felon voting restrictions and race. In the 1985 case, *Hunter v. Underwood*, the U.S. Supreme Court invalidated an Alabama felon disenfranchisement provision based on the original intent of the law. It is

recorded that the purpose of the Alabama law was to "establish white suprem-
acy ... within the limits imposed by the Federal Constitution" (Hench, 1998).
The two-prong test created by Hunter determines whether a felon voting law
violates equal protection intent and impact. According to this test, if a plaintiff
can demonstrate that the law was both penned with racial discriminatory intent and resulted in a racially discriminatory impact, it becomes increasingly
possible to be successful in litigating a felon voting rights case (Price, 2002).

The *Hunter v. Underwood* decision opened the door to assault felon voting bans; however, it is most likely limited to Southern states that continue
to have records and/or laws that show discriminatory intent. After *Hunter v.
Underwood* struck down the part of the Alabama statute specifying crimes of
"**moral turpitude**," the Alabama legislature changed the state law to include
"certain enumerated offenses and all crimes punishable by imprisonment"
(Dugree-Pearson, 2002, p. 393).

Voting Rights Act of 1965

Since the Fourteenth Amendment's Equal Protection Clause appears to have
limited utility in the litigation of felon voting cases, the Voting Rights Act of
1965 has increasingly become a popular mechanism by which to make claims,
or at least arguments, against felony disenfranchisement. After the passage
of the Fifteenth Amendment, many states instituted voting requirements
designed to exclude minorities from voting eligibility (Dugree-Pearson, 2002;
Hench, 1998; Simson, 2002). The Voting Rights Act of 1965 was passed to
circumvent strategies that were created to dilute or deny the minority vote.
The act was particularly focused on Southern states that purposefully eluded
the Fifteenth Amendment through the use of literacy tests (Dugree-Pearson,
2002). The Voting Rights Act served to bolster the Fifteenth Amendment by
barring any "voting qualification ... which results in denial ... of the right ...
to vote on account of race or color" (Hench, 1998).

Section 2 of the act focuses on the racial aspect of **voter dilution**. It prohibits
the use of any "voting qualification or prerequisite to voting, or standard, practice, or procedure ... by any state or political subdivision in a manner which
results in a denial or abridgement of the right of a citizen of the United States
to vote on account of race or color" (Hench, 1998, pp. 744, 746). In 1982, the
VRA was amended to define illegal vote dilution as:

> *If, based on the totality of circumstances, it is shown that the political
> processes leading to the nomination or election in the state or political
> subdivision are not equally open to participation by members of a class of
> citizens protected by [the act] in that its members have less opportunity*

than other members of the electorate to participate in the political process and to elect representatives of their choice (Simson, 2002, p. 60).

As a result of the 1982 amendment, the totality of the circumstances must be considered in Voting Rights Act litigation. The first felon voting rights case after the passage of the 1982 amendment, *Wesley v. Collins* (1986), concerned a Tennessee ex felon who challenged the Tennessee Voting Rights Act by claiming it diluted the voting power of the non-criminal, minority community (Hench, 1998). The Sixth Circuit rejected the argument and held that, although the "totality of circumstances" supported a claim of discrimination, the "facts could not be tied to historical tradition and rationale for the disenfranchisement of felons" (Simson, 2002, p. 61). Therefore, in light of the *Richardson* decision, the Tennessee law was deemed to serve a legitimate and compelling purpose and was thus upheld through the dismissal of the case (Price, 2002).

Since *Wesley*, there have been a number of felon voting rights cases that demonstrate the continued confusion the judiciary has in finding a consistent interpretation of the Voting Rights Act. The discrimination argument has not been very successful. Lower courts are divided on the application of the Voting Rights Act to state felon-voting provisions and inconsistently apply the Fourteenth Amendment (See Box 1.1).

Box 1.1: Key Cases

- Cotton v. Fordice (1988), a Fifth Circuit challenge to Mississippi's felon voting provision, was unsuccessful because the court found "a subsequent legislative reenactment can eliminate the taint from a law that was originally enacted with discriminatory intent."

- *Baker v. Pataki* (1996): The Second Circuit considered the argument that the New York State felon voting statute disparately affected African Americans and Latinos in violation of the Voting Rights Act.

- *Farrakhan v. Washington* (2003), the Ninth Circuit recognized the need for courts to consider the "social and historical conditions" related to felon voting prohibitions, and found that Section 2 of the Voting Rights Act was applicable to the Washington felon voting law.

- *Muntaqim v. Coombe* (2004), the Second Circuit found that the Voting Rights Act is "silent on the topic of felon disenfranchisement" and could not be applied to such laws.

- *Johnson v. Bush* (2005): The Eleventh Circuit court held that considering the Voting Rights Act's application to state felon voting provisions brings up constitutionality issues that the courts have been instructed to avoid.

- *Hayden v. Pataki* (2006): The Second ruled that New York's disenfranchisement law did violate the Voting Rights Act of 1965.

Theoretical Justifications for Felon Disenfranchisement

Retribution

Operates from the vengeance principle that if one violates the law then they lose their right to participate in society.

Subversive Voting

Assumes convicted felons would vote to decriminalize certain behaviors and many harmful crime control policies.

Purity of the Ballot

Presumes that felons "lack virtue" and their criminal behavior indicates they cannot be trusted to vote responsibly.

Electoral Fraud

Suggests that because felons break other laws they will likely commit electoral fraud as well.

Social Contract

Argues that citizens agree to abide by the rules of society in order to reap the benefits of living within that society. When one breaks societal rules they have breached the social contract and are no longer entitled to societal benefits.

Current Felon Disenfranchisement Laws

Historically, felon disenfranchisement has been used by states as an exclusionary tool for certain otherwise eligible voting populations as a collateral "civil" consequence to criminal conviction. This civil consequence is legally deemed as non-penal. Several dominant theoretical explanations provide justification for the continued practice of disenfranchising convicted felons. Further complicating the issue is its persistent status as a states' rights issue in light of the fact that it potentially has a much broader, national, perhaps global impact. Arguably, the United States maintains its classification as a federal nation characterized by having both national and subnational governments (Dye, 1998). In addition, the levels of governments "exercise separate and autonomous authority, both elect their own officials, and both tax their own citizens for the provision of public services" (Dye, 1998, p. 284).

Voting qualifications are the domain of the individual states, so the enfranchisement, disenfranchisement, and reenfranchisement of felony offenders are governed by the state in which they live. Referred to by the U.S. Department of Justice as the "the national crazy quilt of disqualifications and election procedures," the many different felon voting laws and the entities that govern them make it a difficult issue to analyze (Ewald, 2005). Precisely due to the subnational governments, there is no single issue—instead there are fifty.

At the state level, there have been several policy reforms concerning felon-voting rights. These policy changes come in a variety of forms, such as legislation, executive order, or by the creation and subsequent recommendations from appointed task forces. Between 1997 and 2011, there appeared to be a trend toward enfranchising convicted felons. During this period:

- Sixteen states reformed their felon voting provisions through legislation, executive decision, or constitutional amendment;
- Eleven states made their policies less restrictive;
- Four states expanded or enacted a disenfranchisement policy; and
- Two states simplified their restoration processes (The Sentencing Project, 2005).

In 2004, Florida had the highest percentage of disenfranchised voters (9.01%) of any state. Delaware, at 7.54%, was second, and Alabama, at 7.37%, was third. Of these three states, at the time, two them—Florida and Alabama—were permanently disenfranchising states. These two states share a common state constitutional mandate for criminal disenfranchisement with Virginia, Kentucky, and Iowa. In 2004, all five states are considered to be permanently disenfranchising states that require a gubernatorial pardon or executive clemency from the governor or Pardons Board for the restoration of civil rights.

In 2007, the Florida Board of Executive Clemency voted to allow for the automatic restoration of rights for nonviolent felons. In 2011, the decision was reversed, requiring a five-year waiting period for all convicted felons who have completed their sentence (Felony Disenfranchisement Laws, 2011). Similarly,

For more information about current felon disenfranchisement laws, go to:
www.sentencingproject.org

Table 1: State & Federal Totals: Number of Sentenced Prisoners, 2000 & 2008

Offense Category	2000 (% of total)	2008 (% of total)	Change: 2000–2008
Violent	633,740 (47.2%)	730,883 (47.3%)	+ 97,143
Property	256,135 (19.1%)	262,880 (17.0%)	+ 6,745
Drug	338,076 (25.3%)	346,479 (22.4%)	+ 8,403
Public-disorder	104,725 (7.8%)	185,198 (11.9%)	+ 80,473
Other/ unspecified	5,363 (0.4%)	19,194 (1.2%)	+ 13,831
Totals:	**1,338,039** (100%)	**1,544,634** (100%)	**+ 206,595**

in Iowa the gubernatorial pardon requirement was lifted in 2005 when then governor Tom Vilsak issued an executive order retroactively restoring voting rights for ex felons as well as automatic restoration for felons who complete their sentence (Expanding the Vote, 2008). In 2011, the executive order was rescinded by the current governor, Terry Branstad (Felony Disenfranchisement Laws, 2011).

The question of whether or not prison inmates should be allowed to vote is rarely addressed. The following chart shows the total number of prisoners from the years 2000 and 2008. As you see the numbers increase, it becomes increasingly apparent that the numbers of those who are disenfranchised has increased as well. Currently, only two states—Maine and Vermont—allow prison inmates to vote (Felony Disenfranchisement, 2011). Both Utah and Massachusetts allowed prisoners access to the ballot box until 1998 and 2000, respectively (Mauer, 2011b; Felony Disenfranchisement Laws, 2011). Very little research has been done to explain the theory behind disenfranchising prison inmates. The presumption is that inmates have watered-down civil rights, so they are not necessarily entitled to the right to vote.

Mauer (2011b) argues that the public develops its image of a prisoner from social constructions portrayed by the mass media. He also suggests that the public distinguishes prisoners from other offenders, and thus deems them less worthy of retaining civil rights. Prison inmates' loss of voting rights is also seen as an extension of criminal punishment and deserving (Mauer, 2011b). Research on public attitudes finds the general public overwhelmingly support- ive of enfranchisement regardless of correctional status (Dawson-Edwards,

2008). However, prisoners were the least supported, though even their enfranchisement was supported by a majority (Dawson-Edwards, 2008).

Enfranchising inmates would not necessarily end the corollary phenomenon known as **prison-based gerrymandering**—a voter dilution tactic where prisoners are counted in a community that houses the prison (Prisoners of the Census). In other word, prisoners cannot vote (except in Maine or Vermont), so if they are counted for apportionment where they are housed, then they are not counted in the communities where they are from and will likely return to (Prisoners of the Census). Therefore, the community in which the prison is housed gets the political power, which leads to resources, but the community they will return to does not. Prison-based gerrymandering has been equated with the Three-Fifths Compromise of the antebellum South due to its similar ability to dilute and suppress the African American vote (see Chin, 2004).

> For more information about prison-based gerrymandering visit:
> www.prisoners of the census.org

Voter Dilution and
Suppression—*American Blackout*

In order to further grasp how strategies have been used to dilute or suppress the Black vote in the contemporary United States, it is important to understand the historical context of selective enfranchisement in this country. In addition to other tactics, literacy tests and poll taxes have all been used as tactics to sever African Americans from the electorate (Frazier, 2007). Literacy tests, or "intelligence tests," which began in South Carolina in 1882, required the voter to demonstrate his ability to read a certain passage, often a passage from the U.S. Constitution (Race, Voting Rights and Segregation, n. d.). In areas where Blacks and poor whites were equally likely to be illiterate, it has been noted that whites were permitted to recite the passage, though poll workers knew they were unable to read. Black voters were not granted this privilege. Poll taxes, which initiated in Georgia in 1871, required prospective voters to pay a $1–2 per year tax to vote (Race, Voting Rights and Segregation, n. d.). This was also problematic given the fact that the newly emancipated had never earned a wage as slaves and were often very poor and unable to pay the tax. In the early 1900s, poll taxes were adopted in most states with a substantial population of freedmen (Hench, 1998). These taxes quickly diminished.

Felon disenfranchisement literature has repeatedly revealed that, like poll taxes and literacy tests, felon disenfranchisement is a policy that looks race neutral, but discriminatory intentions are well documented. Unlike the race neutral, but racist, direct disenfranchisement tactics, felon disenfranchisement is an indirect tactic, which makes it even harder to prove intentional racial discrimination.

> For more information on U.S. historic
> direct disenfranchisement practices, visit:
> www.umich.edu/~lawrace/disenfranchise1.htm

Voter Dilution

The development of impoverished, predominantly African American communities can be linked to the post–Civil War era. The internal migration patterns of African- Americans can be traced directly to the movement of former slaves and their offspring to the North, in search of better opportunities.

Facing the immediate aftermath of the Civil War, freed slaves commonly lived in integrated communities (Wilson, 1973). Around 1890, the composition of mixed-race neighborhoods began to shift, as many African-Americans were forced, through residential segregation, to relocate through such mechanisms as "neighborhood improvement associations, economic boycotts … acts of violence and … restrictive covenants" (Spear, 1971, p. 159; Wilson, 1973, p. 104). African American residents maintain the majority of these resulting neighborhoods at a rate of approximately 20 to 1 (Clear & Cadora, 2003). One's social location is absolutely impacted by his/her spatial location, which can be a determinant of the social opportunities afforded to an individual. As Clear and Cadora (2003) suggest, "place matters in life" (p. 9).

The suppression of political participation prevents members of a community from influencing public policy. Communities with lower voting rates have been shown to have higher incarceration rates (Uggen & Manza, 2004). This is at least partially due to the fact that individuals with a felony arrest are less likely to vote. Incarcerated individuals are 27 percent less likely to vote, when that right is afforded them, than non-incarcerated individuals. Even when incarcerated individuals are not located within a community, their votes would have a significant impact there. Such self-imposed political suppression is exacerbated by officially enforced political suppression. In neighborhoods with diminished internal resources, increased political capacity may be a significant tool for soliciting external resources (Bennett, 1995).

According to Roberts (2004), mass incarceration "translates the denial of individual felon's voting rights into the disenfranchisement of entire communities" (Clear, 2007, p. 114). Cardinale (2004) found that the disenfranchisement of homeless ex felons reportedly caused feelings of being "a fraction of a citizen" (p. 7). He suggested that this information be used to provide an understanding of "how disenfranchisement influences people's views of themselves and the legitimacy of politics in general" (p. 7).

Wahler's (2006) study of Kentucky parolee perceptions of felon voting restrictions yielded similar results. The parolees discussed a desire for participation in the political system and frustration with their political marginalization. One parolee stated:

> ... *now I have kids and I want to do the right thing. Plus, I want to have a say in what happens around me. I don't like the President and the government now and I didn't get to vote to say what's happening. ... If I don't vote, then I can't complain about it, I guess ...* (Wahler, 2006, p. 13).

King and Mauer (2004), in *The Vanishing Black Electorate*, examine the state and local impacts of these laws, focusing specifically on areas with higher levels of disenfranchised individuals. Their findings highlight the need to provide a voice for the voiceless. One in eight Black males is disenfranchised in the state of Georgia. In Atlanta, one in seven Black males cannot vote due to felony disenfranchisement laws. Zips codes with high concentrations of convicted felons have more prominent voter dilution. Additional data also suggests that felon voting prohibitions result in voter dilution.

Black males, however, are not just individually impacted. There is evidence that the political power of others in their communities is also affected (see Lynch & Sabol, 2001). King and Mauer reported that "given the concentration of felony disenfranchisement in primarily African-American communities, persons who have not been convicted of a felony are affected through the diminished strength of their political voice" (2004, p. 15).

Political candidates focus on areas they believe have the potential for the most voter support (King and Mauer, 2004). The effect of disenfranchisement on the diminished political strength and its "chilling effect on political

In an October 2006 study, the League of Women Voters in Kentucky conducted an assessment of such dilution in the Commonwealth. They found that one in seventeen Kentucky citizens is disenfranchised due to a felony conviction. The study also found that Kentucky has the sixth highest disenfranchisement rate in the United States. Additionally, 90 percent of those disenfranchised in Kentucky are not imprisoned, and two thirds have completed their sentences (League of Women Voters, 2006). Lastly, the study found that one in four African Americans in Kentucky is disenfranchised due to felony convictions, which is triple the national rate for African American felony disenfranchisement.

engagement of certain neighborhoods" make it unlikely that candidates will campaign in areas compromised by felon voting laws (King & Mauer, p. 15). Because the electoral campaign is the point at which candidates are often most open to talk with constituents, this indifference is harmful for low-income or minority-populated communities. According to King and Mauer (2004), as the prison population continues to increase, the voice of residents in these communities will continue to diminish due to felony disenfranchisement and subsequent community isolation. Brown-Dean (2003) captured this sentiment well when she stated: "the cumulative impact of these statutes simultaneously dilutes the full development of African-American political equality and American democracy by reinforcing the politics of exclusion" (p. 15).

Voter Suppression

Research spurred by the Florida election procedures and results in the 2000 presidential elections yielded information that thousands were disenfranchised because of actual felony convictions or the fraudulent placement of innocent names of felon voter lists (King & Mauer, 2004). Congresswoman Cynthia McKinney conducted hearings with Choice Point, the company contracted by the state of Florida to develop the felon voter list. Ultimately, the company admitted to misidentifying 90,000 voters as felons ineligible to vote. Other hearings with then governor Jeb Bush and representatives from the Florida Board of Elections provided substantial evidence that officials were indifferent to the misidentification of names. According to *American Blackout* (2006), Governor Bush ordered 50,000 names removed from the eligible voter lists five months before the election. Most of these names were African American or Hispanic persons.

This mass disenfranchisement potentially caused an unconstitutional impact on the Florida election results, which may have subsequently affected the presidency (Simson, 2002; Uggen & Manza, 2004). As a result, a series of lawsuits filed by groups such as the National Association for the Advancement of Colored People (NAACP) and the American Civil Liberties Union (ACLU) have challenged the fairness of Florida's voting system, citing the 600,000 Florida ex felons who are ineligible to vote though their sentences are complete (Glanton, 2004). Referred to as a "Jim Crow" or "apartheid" election, George W. Bush won the presidency by a mere 537 votes.

Since then, several studies have been conducted to explore the electoral impact that felon voting prohibitions have on U.S. presidential and Senate elections. Sociologists Jeff Manza and Christopher Uggen have extensively studied the electoral impact of disenfranchised felons by extracting data from the *Survey of State Prison Inmates* and estimating the voting behavior of felons based on the demographic data of their non-incarcerated counterparts (Manza

& Uggen, 2002; Uggen & Manza, 2004). Their two analyses considered both the total criminally disenfranchised population and separate correctional statuses—ex felon, probation, and parole.

In 2002, they sought to discover "whether felon disenfranchisement has had meaningful political consequences in past elections" by examining the possible election outcomes in a hypothetical situation where all disenfranchised felons could vote from 1992–2000 election data (Uggen & Manza, 2002, p. 782). For presidential elections, they approximated participation from 35% of felons. For senate elections in "nonpresidential election" years, they estimated participation from 24% of disenfranchised felons (p. 786). For both types of elections, the theoretical felon voters demonstrated a strong alliance with the Democratic Party. The alliance was more pronounced in presidential elections, but it was concluded that felon voting prohibitions have given the Republican Party a minimal, but apparent, lead in each presidential and senatorial election in the study. Overall, they found that the inclusion of the entire disenfranchised felon population made a significant impact, but when correctional statuses were considered independently, it appeared that non-incarcerated felons, who make up the bulk of the disenfranchised, likely had a greater impact on Democratic election losses (Uggen & Manza, 2002).

In 2004, they expanded their previous research and included data from 1978–2000. Similar, but modified, research methods were used, and they focused on "whether the disenfranchisement of non-incarcerated felons have any practical impact on American electoral politics?" (Manza & Uggen, 2004, p. 497). The study validated their previous findings on the 2000 presidential election and provided new evidence suggesting that three Senate elections could have also been affected by the absent votes of convicted felons (Manza & Uggen, 2004). For the 2000 presidential election, they found that an estimated 27.2% of Florida's 613,514 disenfranchised felons would have voted (Manza & Uggen, 2004). More specifically, an estimated 63,542 would have voted Democratic (Manza & Uggen, 2004).

Additionally, Manza and Uggen (2004) pinpointed three Senate elections that would have had different results—Virginia 1978, Kentucky 1984, and Kentucky 1998. In 1984, Republican Mitch McConnell beat Democrat Walter Huddleston. Twenty years later, Mitch McConnell still holds a seat in the U.S. Senate, representing the Commonwealth of Kentucky. Additionally, or ironically, he has been a stark opponent to felon voting rights. In 2002, in his opposing comments to the proposed Civic Participation and Rehabilitation Act, he declared, "States have a significant interest in reserving the vote for those who have abided by the social contract … Those that break our laws should not dilute the vote of law-abiding citizens" (Behrens, Uggen, & Manza, 2003, p. 571). This statement exemplifies his disdain for granting the franchise to convicted felons.

The impact of Kentucky's felon disenfranchisement law was specifically studied in 2008 when Shutt and colleagues analyzed its effects on the presidential and senatorial election results (Vito, Shutt, & Tewksbury, 2009). A survey of probationer and parolees was used to estimate the voting preferences of the population. They found that Kentucky probationers and parolees tended to lean toward Democratic candidates and would have favored Obama (54.7 percent) over McCain (32.3 percent). However, in contrast to the Manza and Uggen (2004) research, the addition of disenfranchised under community supervision would not change the final results of the state—McCain would have still carried Kentucky in the 2008 presidential election. As it relates to the senatorial election, U.S. senator Mitch McConnell would have prevailed; however, the hypothetical felon voters favored Bruce Lunsford by a margin of 41.8 to 28.6 percent (Vito et al., 2009).

Senator McConnell's opposition of the federal felon voting bill seems to be in contrast to what his home state and other states have done in recent years. The result of such staggering statistics, legal challenges, and research projects has seemingly sparked a trend in reevaluating state voter eligibility requirements. Since the 2000 election, nine states have reduced the stringency of their felon voting laws, thus allowing more convicted felons to vote. Others have streamlined the restoration process to make it easier for convicted felons to regain their voting rights. A recent shift has been detected in state felon voting practices. In 2011, both Iowa and Florida rescinded practices that prevented lifetime disenfranchisement for ex felons.

Conclusion

Any discussion on race and felon disenfranchisement must consider the political context of the issue, and must be interfaced with the effects of the post–Civil War conditions in America. Countless documents show that the current racial impact of felon voting restrictions can be directly linked back to their reported discriminatory intent. Even corollary issues such as unreliable felon voting lists (i.e., Florida) and prison-based gerrymandering exist as a direct result of felon disenfranchisement laws. The question remains: How can this be? How can we still consciously use tactics to "protect the purity of the ballot box" in our contemporary and civilized society? In the United States, voter dilution and suppression have been outlawed in every form other than as a disparate result of racially neutral state disenfranchisement laws. Hidden as indirect disenfranchisement, felon voting prohibitions in effect achieve the same goals as their unlawful direct disenfranchising counterparts—poll taxes and literacy tests. However, felon disenfranchisement laws remain shrouded in protection by the Fourteenth Amendment while millions of citizens suffer from civil death and their communities suffer as collateral damage.

References

A.L. Const. § 182 (1901).

Bennett, S. F. (1995). Community organizations and crime. *Annals of the American Academy of Political and Social Science*, 539, 72–84.

Behrens, A. (2004). Voting—not quite a fundamental right? A look at the legal and legislative challenges to felon disenfranchisement law. *Minnesota Law Review* 89, 231.

Behrens, A., Uggen, C., & Manza, J. (2003). Ballot manipulation and the "menace of negro domination": Racial threat and felon disenfranchisement in the United States, 1850–2002. *American Journal of Sociology*, 109 (3), 559–605.

Cardinale, M. (2004). *Triple Decker Disenfranchisement: First Person Accounts of Losing the Right to Vote Among Poor, Homeless Americans with a Felony Conviction.* The Sentencing Project. Available online at: www.sentencingproject.org

Chin, G. J. (2004). Reconstruction, felon disenfranchisement, and the right to vote: Did the Fifteenth Amendment repeal Section 2 of the Fourteenth Amendment? *Georgetown Law Journal, 92,* 259.

Clear, T. R. (2007). *Imprisoning Communities: How Mass Incarceration Makes Disadvantaged Neighborhoods Worse.* New York: Oxford University Press.

Clear, T. R., & Cadora, E. (2003). *Community Justice.* Belmont, CA: Wadsworth.

Collier v. Menzel, 221 Cal. Rpt. 110, (Ct. App. 1985).

Dawson-Edwards, C. (2008). Enfranchising convicted felons: Current research on opinions toward felon voting rights. *Journal of Offender Rehabilitation*, 46 (3/4). [Reprinted in D. Phillips, ed., *Probation and Parole: Current Issues.* New York: Routledge, 2008].

Dawson-Edwards, C. (2011). Politics, Policy and DMC Communities: The Cyclical Impact of Community Political Disempowerment on DMC. In N. Parsons-Pollard (ed.). *Disproportionate Minority Contact.* Durham, NC: Carolina Academic Press.

Doe v. Rowe, 156 F. Supp. 2d 35, 56 (2001).

Du Bois, W. E. B. (1899/1973). *The Philadelphia Negro: A Social Study.* Millwood, NY: Kraus-Thomson Organization Limited.

Du Bois, W. E. B. (1901). The spawn of slavery. *The Missionary Review of the World, 14,* 737–745.

Du Bois, W. E. B. (1935). *Black Reconstruction in America.* New York: Harcourt, Brace & Company.

Dugree-Pearson, T. (2002). Disenfranchisement—A race neutral punishment for felony offenders or way to diminish the minority vote? *Hamline Journal of Public Law & Policy,* 23, 359.

Dye, T. R. (1998). *Understanding Public Policy* (9th ed.). Upper Saddle River, NJ: Prentice-Hall.

Ewald, A. (2005). *A Crazy Quilt of Tiny Pieces: State and Local Administration of American Criminal Disenfranchisement Law.* The Sentencing Project. Available online at: www.sentencingproject.org

Fellner, J., & Mauer, M. (1998). Losing the vote: The impact of felony disenfranchisement laws in the United States. Human Rights Watch & the Sentencing Commission. Available at: http://www.hrw.org/reports98/vote

Frazier, C. N. (2007). Removing the Vestiges of Discrimination: Criminal Disenfranchisement Laws and Strategies for Challenging Them. *Kentucky Law Journal,* 95, 481.

Glanton, D. (2004, July 28). Restoring felons' voting rights a heated election-year issue in Fla., *Chicago Tribune.* Retrieved on October, 29, 2004, at www.kentucky.com

Green v. Board of Elections, 380 F. 2d 445 (2nd Cir. 1967)

Hench, V. E. (1998). The death of voting rights: The legal disenfranchisement of minority voters. *Case Western Reserve,* 48, 777.

Hunter v. Underwood, 471 U.S. 222 (1985).

Johnson-Parris, A. S. (2003). Felon disenfranchisement: The unconscionable social contract breached. *Virginia Law Review, 89,* 109.

King, R. S., & Mauer, M. (2004). The Vanishing Black Electorate: Felony Disenfranchisement in Atlanta, Georgia. The Sentencing Project. Available [online] at: www.sentencingproject.org

League of Women Voters. (2006). Felony Disenfranchisement in the Commonwealth of Kentucky: A Report of the League of Women Voters of Kentucky. The Sentencing Project.

Lynch, J. P., & Sabol, W. J. (2001). Prisoner Reentry in Perspective. The Urban Institute. Available online at: www.urban.org/uploadedPDF/410213_reentry.pdf

Manza, J., Brooks, C., & Uggen, C. (2002). "Civil death" or civil rights? Attitudes towards felon disenfranchisement in the United States. WP-02-39.

Manza, J., Brooks, C., & Uggen, C. (2004). Public attitudes toward felon disenfranchisement in the United States. *Public Opinion Quarterly,* 68 (2): 275–286.

Manza, J., & Uggen, C. (2002). Democratic contradiction? The political consequences of felon disenfranchisement. *American Sociological Review,* 67, 777–803.

Manza, J., & Uggen, C. (2006). *Locked Out: Felon Disenfranchisement and American Democracy.* New York: Oxford University Press.

Mauer, M. (2011a). Addressing racial disparities in incarceration. *The Prison Journal,* 91(3), 87S–101S.

Mauer, M. (2011b). Voting behind bars: An argument for voting by prisoners. *Howard Law Journal,* 54(3), 549–560.

Murphree v. Winter, 589 F. Supp. 374 (1984).

Price, M. (2002). Addressing ex felon disenfranchisement: legislation vs. litigation. *Journal of Law and Policy,* 11; 369.

Prisoners of the Census. Available online at: http://felonvoting.procon.org/view.resource.php?resourceID=004339

Race, Voting Rights, and Segregation (n. d.). http://www.umich.edu/~lawrace/disenfran-chise1.htm

Richardson v. Ramirez, 418 U.S. 24 (1974).

Roberts, J. V. (1992). Public opinion, crime and criminal justice, pp. 99–180. In M. Tonry (ed.), *Crime and Justice: A Review of Research*. Chicago: University of Chicago Press.

Rose, D. R. (1995). Fighting back against crime and disorder: An examination of neigh-borhood based organizations and social disorganization theory. Unpublished disserta-tion, Department of Sociology, Duke University, Durham, NC.

Rose, J. C. (1906). Negro suffrage: The constitutional point of view. *American Political Science Review, 1* (17), 25–27.

Sabol, W. J., West, H. C., & Cooper, M. (2010). *Prisoners in 2008*. Washington, DC: Bureau of Justice Statistics, U.S. Department of Justice.

Simson, E. (2002). Justice denied: How felony disenfranchisement laws undermine American democracy. Americans for Democratic Action Education Fund. Available online at: www.adaction.org

Spear, A. (1971). The origins of the urban ghetto, 1870–1915. In N. I. Huggins, M. Kilson, & D. M. Fox (eds.). *Key Issues in the Afro-American Experience*. New York: Harcourt Brace Jovanovich, Inc.

Special Project. (1970). Collateral Consequences of a Criminal Conviction, *Vanderbilt Law Review, 23*, p. 929.

Stephens v. Yeomans, 327 F. Supp. 1182, (D.N.J. 1970).

The Sentencing Project (November 2005). Felony disenfranchisement laws in the United States. Available online at: http://www.sentencingproject.org/pdfs/1046.pdf

The Sentencing Project (March 2011). Felony disenfranchisement laws in the United States. Available online at: http://www.sentencingproject.org/detail/publication.cfm?publication_id=15&id=131

Thompson, M. E. (2002). Don't do the crime if you ever intend to vote again: Challenging disenfranchisement of ex felons as cruel and unusual punishment. *Seton Hall Law Review, 33,* 167.

U.S. Const. Amend. XV, § 1.

U.S. v. Andrews, 462 F.2d 914, 917, (1st Cir. 1972)

Vito, G. F., Shutt, J. E., & Tewksbury, R. (2009). Estimating the Impact of Kentucky's Felon Disenfranchisement Policy on 2008 Presidential and Senatorial Elections. *Federal Probation*, 73(1).

Wahler, E. (2006). Losing the right to vote: Perceptions of permanent disenfranchise-ment and the civil rights restoration application process in the state of Kentucky. The Sentencing Project. Available [online] at: http://www.sentencingproject.org/pdfs/ky-losingtherighttovote.pdf

Wilson, W. J. (1973). *Power, Racism, and Privilege: Race Relations in Theoretical and Sociopolitical Perspectives*. New York: Free Press.

Learn More on the Internet:

The Sentencing Project: Voting Rights:
   http://www.sentencingproject.org/template/page.cfm?id=133
American Blackout:
   http://video.google.com/videoplay?docid=-5965670944815984616#

Discussion Questions:

1. Is voting a right or a privilege? Does this distinction matter?
2. Should the states continue to be allowed to decide whether or not ex offenders vote, or should the federal government mandate that all those who have served their sentences be allowed to vote?

CREDITS

Hon. Peggy Fulton Hora, "The Ten Key Components of Drug Courts," *Substance Use and Misuse*, vol. 37, no. 12–13. Copyright © 2002 by Informa Healthcare. Reprinted with permission.

Michael Thompson, Dr. Fred Osher, and Denise Tomasini-Joshi, "The Ten Essential Elements of Mental Health Courts," *Improving Responses to People with Mental Illnesses: The Essential Elements of a Mental Health Court*, pp. 1–10. Copyright © 2007 by Council of State Governments Justice Center. Reprinted with permission.